Administering library service in the elementary school

Books are fun to share.

SECOND EDITION

Administering library service in the

elementary school

by JEWEL GARDINER

*Librarian, Professional Library, and
Supervisor, Elementary and Junior
High School Libraries,
Sacramento City Unified School District
Sacramento, California*

AMERICAN LIBRARY ASSOCIATION

Chicago 1954

Copyright 1954 by the American Library Association

Library of Congress catalog card number 53-12719

Manufactured in the United States of America

TO *school librarians everywhere*

whose happy privilege it is

to build lasting friendships

between children and books

From the preface to the first edition

The administration and organization of an elementary school library involves vastly more than the mastery of library technics. It involves the skillful coordination of three distinct fields—the field of librarianship, the field of teaching, and the field of school administration. Consequently, this book is addressed not to school librarians alone but to all persons whose work bears an intimate relationship to the success of the elementary school library program. It is addressed to superintendents, to principals, to teacher-librarians, to classroom teachers, to librarians in public libraries, to instructors in library schools.

It is, of course, addressed first of all to elementary school librarians, because they have charge of the libraries and deal firsthand with the various problems which are discussed. Those with limited experience or limited professional training will find helpful the discussion of definite procedures involved in setting up and maintaining a library. Even those with the best professional library training may be aided in their work by the analysis of problems in the fields of elementary education and educational administration which are involved in the administration of the library program.

The book is addressed also to others who have a vital relationship to the library program. It can be useful to superintendents who employ librarians, assign people to library work, and who establish, equip, and maintain libraries. It will assist elementary school principals in their understanding of the elementary school library program. Their understanding of the problems involved and their attitudes probably have more to do with the effective functioning of the elementary school library than any other group. It will help classroom teachers to cooperate intelligently with the library. It will aid librarians in public libraries who are engaged in providing library service to elementary schools and are seeking to cooperate with teachers and school librarians.

Finally, the book is addressed to instructors in library schools engaged in training elementary school librarians, since many of the problems involved in administering elementary school library service are not confined to the field of library technics but merge into the fields of elementary education and school administration.

JEWEL GARDINER
LEO B. BAISDEN

Preface to the second edition

The new edition does not deviate from the original edition in basic views concerning the purposes and activities of the elementary school library. In the intervening years there has been an increasing acceptance of the library as an essential element in the elementary school. The literature in the field has increased tremendously, and merely by investigating it one discovers that administrators, principals, supervisors, college professors, teachers, and children's authors, as well as librarians, have made worthwhile contributions. It is noteworthy that the Department of Elementary School Principals of the National Education Association devoted its thirtieth yearbook (1951) to *Elementary School Libraries Today*. A comparison of this yearbook with the twelfth yearbook (1933) entitled *Elementary School Libraries* gives a quick picture of the rapid development of the elementary school library. The library is now accepted as an integral part of the elementary school.

While a few chapters from the original edition have been retained with relatively little revision—for instance, the chapters on personnel, the library in the primary grades, and cooperation with the public library—a large part of the book has been entirely rewritten. New material has been added on publicity, radio, television, bibliotherapy, guidance, pupil assistants, and citizenship. The library as a materials center receives full treatment. All references have been brought up to date.

The author has greatly missed the guidance and inspiration of Leo B. Baisden, the co-author of the original edition, whose untimely death occurred just as that edition came from the press.

December, 1953   JEWEL GARDINER

Acknowledgments

Acknowledgment was made in the first edition to the following persons whose interest and assistance contributed to the writing of the book:

To Miss Mabel Gillis, then Librarian of the California State Library, and Mrs. Eleanor Hitt Morgan, then Assistant Librarian of the California State Library, for the inspiration of their leadership in the development of school libraries.

To Miss Helen Heffernan, Assistant Division Chief, Elementary Education, California State Department of Education, for her active leadership in the development of elementary school libraries and for her encouragement in undertaking the writing of a book in this field.

To Mrs. Grace Taylor Dean, Librarian of the Sacramento Public Library, for her keen understanding of the possibilities of cooperation between the public library and the school library.

The interest of these persons in school libraries has continued and the author again gratefully acknowledges her indebtedness to them. She also wishes to express her thanks to others who have assisted with the new edition:

To Miss Jessie Boyd, Director of Libraries, Oakland City Schools, who read the entire manuscript and offered many helpful suggestions.

To Mrs. Pauline Love, Chief, Publishing Department, and to Miss Mildred Batchelder, Executive Secretary, Division of Libraries for Children and Young People, of the American Library Association, for their encouragement and help.

To Miss Betty Jane Powell for her contribution in the preparation of the manuscript.

xi

To the schools of Pittsburgh, Pa., Richmond, Va., Cleveland, Ohio, Baltimore, Md., Bloomington, Minn., Newton, Mass., Evanston, Ill., Chicago, Ill., Burbank, Long Beach, Los Angeles, Oakland, and Sacramento, Calif., for photographs which picture vividly some of the ideas expressed in this book, and to Mrs. Rachel de Angelo, Executive Secretary, American Association of School Librarians, of the American Library Association, for her assistance in securing the photographs. To my own nieces and nephew, Cathy, Debby, Vickie and Gardy de Back, for the frontispiece which depicts so clearly the fun of sharing books.

To Miss Bernice Braden, Consultant in Library Science, Sacramento City Schools, for the sketches of bulletin board displays.

And to the teacher-librarians of the elementary schools of Sacramento for the inspiration of their work in the elementary school library field and for the fact that they have constantly exemplified in their work so many of the ideals, activities and practices presented in this book, she will ever remain grateful.

Contents

Illustrations

There is wonder in the story hour.

*Time out for getting acquainted
with the great.*

chapter **1**

Children and the

world of books

Paradise, for me, would be a place where the workers of all time might come together, to talk about their labor on this earth, no matter what eons of time once actually separated them: a kind of 'High Tor' where lovers of like things may find each other in understanding; where Michelangelo receives Renoir, and Beethoven, with unlocked ears, gives welcome to the least musician, recently arrived."[1] Thus spoke Frances Clarke Sayers on an occasion of the awarding of the John Newbery Medal.

To children as to adults the library verily is such a paradise—what riches are here, what romance, what thrill, what roads to wander, what heights to ascend, what people to know. It would seem that there could be no more profound educational purpose than the aim to lead children into this paradise of books, so that from earliest childhood children and books are brought together in constant and happy association. It is not enough for schools merely to "teach children how to read." Far more significant is the necessity of furnishing them something worth while in order that they may read. Today there is a most wonderful and fascinating field of children's books. There are books on every level from the kindergarten picture books to the delightful books for older boys and girls. There

---

[1] Frances Clarke Sayers, "Lose Not the Nightingale," *A.L.A. Bulletin,* XXXI (October 1937), 621-28.

1

are books for every childhood interest and books to meet every whim, hobby, or fancy. There are books which are works of art in every sense of the word, which are beautiful examples of printing and bookmaking and which contain exquisite pictures by the finest of artists. Great as this field of children's books is, it is being increased constantly by a stream of new books.

It matters not how great the supply of children's books if a child cannot get his hands on them; for him they may as well not exist. One of the most important problems facing parents, teachers, and librarians today is how to bring the world of children and the world of books together. Books cost money. Few families can afford large numbers of books. Many families live too far from a public library to make full use of its resources for children. Many parents, unfortunately, are unaware of the part books might play in the lives of their children. This situation is a challenge especially to the school and to the public library to seek the most effective means of providing books for all children and of giving such instruction in the use of books and libraries as will make for a permanent and happy association.

The greatest single factor in developing interest in books and the habit of reading is the accessibility of books. The child who has difficulty in getting books will naturally read little, and his fields of reading experience and reading interest must consequently remain limited. The child who has constant access to good books has the opportunity to develop through reading one of the most important intellectual and recreational outlets he can ever know.

In seeking to make books available for all children, the home, the school, and the public library all have a part to play. It is the part of the home to encourage in the child pride in the ownership of books. The child's personal library may be small but it is his, and on this foundation of pride his interest in books may be built. Librarians may assist parents by giving advice as to the kinds of books to be purchased. This may help to make the child's personal book collection something worthy of being cherished. The elementary school is in a position to make a great contribution to children's interests in books by making good books available to all children every day of the school year. In fact, for many children there will be no other regular source of books. It is for this reason that every elementary school, regardless of its size, should have its own library or classroom book collection. It is to this library the child should look for all essential reference materials he may need in connection with his schoolwork and for good books to read for pleasure and recreation. The school should afford some opportunity for him to practice every day the art of reading, which teachers are struggling so diligently to teach in the reading period. However expert the instruction in the formal reading program, the child must in the last analysis learn to read for himself. He alone can acquire skill in the art of reading, and this only through constant opportunities to read.

While school libraries should make books available for school use, many elementary schools do not have sufficient funds to make books available for home circulation. It is here that the obligation falls heavily on the public library. The time available for library activities during the school day does not provide most children sufficient time for the amount of leisure reading which they might do with pleasure and profit. Children should have books under circumstances which provide time for leisurely reading. Probably the most important and universal use of books for both children and adults is for recreational purposes. It is difficult to name any other human resource which is potentially so rich as a recreational outlet. The public library seeks to meet this need by providing books for home circulation to boys and girls.

The functional school library furnishes children a constant supply of books and library materials to meet all educational needs. It provides both an adequate and well-selected collection of books for recreational reading, and a collection of reference books and materials suitable for the curriculum of the school. It provides for individual differences. It gives opportunity for children to discuss books and share their reading experiences. It provides a wide collection of supplementary books and materials for circulation to classrooms. The school library program includes instruction in the use of books and libraries so that children become skillful in using library facilities in general, and thus may find their ways easily and happily in the world of books. Children who have the privilege of using books and libraries as a regular part of their educational experience can never look upon the library as a mysterious, distant, or forbidding place but will find it an open path to fields and woodlands filled with sunlight and leading to the land of heart's desire.

chapter 2

The function of the library in
the modern elementary school

The elementary school library is a comparatively recent educational development. While the library has always held an important place in secondary and collegiate education, it is only now coming to be widely accepted as an essential feature of the elementary school. This situation has been the result of tradition and not of educational planning. When the American high school was developed, it followed the tradition of the academy and of the college in the general plan of organization and instruction and consequently the library became, from the beginning, an important feature of the high school. But the American elementary school arose from a different tradition.

From its inception, the function of the elementary school was assumed to be the teaching from textbooks of certain skill subjects, the so-called "fundamental subjects." The entire educational program, including school organization, teaching methods, and teaching materials, centered about these subjects. The textbook held a central place in this type of learning, and the methodology was based on assigning lessons in textbooks and hearing recitations. In this type of school there was little occasion to use materials from sources outside the textbook. While such a school sometimes had a so-called "library," it played no essential part in the educational program. It ordinarily consisted of a nondescript collection of books, unorganized, uncataloged, and poorly selected for children. Such libraries served principally as book depositories from which children might withdraw books to take home, but seldom did they perform any of the more vital functions which a modern elementary school library performs.[1]

Why the elementary school library?

The modern elementary school has a new type of curriculum. The study-recitation type of procedure, adapted only to textbook and memoriter learning, has given way to an active, integrated curriculum involving social and dynamic classroom procedures. Recent courses of study in such subjects as social studies, reading, and science indicate clearly this shift in emphasis. Many of the newer courses are developed about "units of work" or "areas of learning" in which the learning process is so coordinated and integrated that old subject lines often completely disappear. The information needed for carrying out such courses of study involves the widest field of reading and reference materials—textbooks, library books, magazines, pamphlets, maps, charts, pictures, and visual materials. In any educational program where knowledge is no longer considered as confined to the pages of textbooks, children need a vast variety of reference materials if their minds are to be opened to the living world about them. They need to acquire skill in seeking information through various channels and to become familiar with reference and library resources. They also need access to a wide variety of literature—both fiction and nonfiction. In order to meet the needs of such an educational program, library service is as essential in the modern elementary school as in the high school or college. The service differs, of course, in the sense that simpler materials must be provided. Children in the primary grades are able to use library resources only in a restricted sense. However, as children progress through the elementary grades they become increasingly capable of utilizing all types of library resources. In the upper grades they are able to make extensive use of reference sources, they have wider reading interests and they are able to carry on research in ever widening fields of intellectual interests.

---

[1] A good summary of the development of elementary school library service is given by Hazelle M. Anderson in "Service at the Elementary Level," *Library Trends,* I (January 1953), 298-310.

Varied functions

The elementary school library is an essential element of the school program and the basic purpose of the library is identical with the basic purpose of the school it serves. Its unique function is to provide the varied library services and activities required by the modern educational program. Among the well-recognized services to be provided are the following:

> An adequate and well-selected collection of books for recreational and free reading
>
> A suitable collection of reference books and materials
>
> Reference and supplementary materials for classroom use
>
> A suitable collection of audio-visual materials
>
> Instruction in the use of books and libraries suitable to the age and development of the children
>
> Guidance in reading and in the development of reading habits and tastes
>
> Opportunities to discuss books and share in reading experiences

Such services when properly executed provide for individual differences through a book collection which includes books on all subjects and varying greatly in reading difficulty. Through opportunity for children to share their reading experiences, new interests are developed and satisfactory personal adjustments are made. Children become skillful in using library facilities in general through planned activities which include instruction in the use of books and libraries. They become discriminating users of printed and audio-visual materials. Thus the library meets the needs of pupils and teachers. Thus does it help boys and girls to develop satisfying interests and hobbies, and thus do they come to consider the public library as a means of continuing education and cultural life.

The library—a materials center

Although schools have always stressed the verbal as the most important process of learning, the modern school is placing much emphasis upon "seeing" and "experiencing" in the learning process. The new emphasis may necessitate the extension of elementary school library service to include these new phases of learning. Some elementary school libraries are called upon to offer extended services which include the housing, circulation, and effective utilization of audio-visual materials of all types. These materials include films, filmstrips, slides, recordings, transcriptions, maps, charts, globes, machines for projection, screens, models, and realia of all types. The library is the one agency in the school organized to handle efficiently materials which are circulated throughout the school, and so the library quite naturally becomes the dynamic "Materials Center," "Resource Center," or "Instructional Aids Center" of the school.

When such additional responsibilities are assigned to the library, principals should be certain that adequate provisions are made to aid the librarian in handling the materials successfully. This will require both special facilities for housing the materials and special clerical help or other assistants. The librarian of this type of materials center will need to become well informed about all the materials since it will become her responsibility to help teachers in the selection and proper utilization of them. A new type of training for the prospective school librarian is needed in order to make her as expert in the selection, handling, and effective use of audio-visual materials as she is in the field of printed materials. A new type of planning for the physical setup of the library is being developed. Not only are special shelving and other types of space needed for the housing of nonprinted materials but noise-free preview or "listening" rooms are becoming as essential to the library as are conference rooms.

Many school libraries will not be called upon to give service in nonprinted materials since many cities and counties maintain special audio-visual education departments under the direction of a special supervisor or director. This central agency ordinarily is responsible for notifying teachers of new materials, conferring with them about materials suitable for use with particular units of work or courses of study, and it has full charge of circulation of materials to individual schools or teachers. In this type of organization the library sometimes serves as a clearinghouse for all such materials. If the library serves in this capacity, special clerical assistance will be needed to handle the clerical details involved in receiving, distributing, and returning materials.

The library in relation to radio and television

Radio broadcasting is one of the most powerful and significant mediums of communication. It now enters most homes and is utilized effectively in many schools. Educational programs designed for school use bring enrichment and information to students in classrooms in such fields as social studies, science, music, and literature. Radio has become a dynamic educational force.

Many schools provide radios as a part of standard classroom equipment. Others provide portable radios for circulation to classrooms as needed. Sometimes these portable radios are circulated through the principal's office, but often they are housed in the library and circulated from there.

Librarians need to be alert to the possibilities of utilization of radio in connection with the program of library activities. Very good storytelling programs, book reviews, book quiz programs, author interviews, and dramatizations of children's books are available over networks and on local stations. Such programs can be used very successfully in the library for listening and for class activities. Some audio-visual education departments make tape recordings of programs for future use in classrooms. Transcriptions of many children's programs are also available for purchase. Radio programs, either as "live programs," transcriptions, or tape recordings, can form the basis for stimulating discussions of books, authors, illustrators, and reading in general.

A "Radio Corner" on the bulletin board may list outstanding children's programs, giving both the stations and hours, for out-of-school as well as for in-school programs, and may suggest books for reading in connection with the programs.

As television continues to be used for educational purposes, it will certainly have an effect on the elementary school library. School and children's librarians report that TV has been a great influence in widening children's interests and has affected their book requests. Many school and public libraries report that books on puppets, both on the adult and children's levels, have had a much wider circulation since TV puppet shows have become so popular. The excellent science shows, such as "Zoo Parade" and "Living Wonders," have brought many more requests for authentic science books. Librarians in the entire area covered by television station KING, Seattle, Washington, report more reading by children since the station began "Telaventure Tales," a once-a-week, thirty-minute program, initiated in November, 1951. This program began as a test sponsored by the station, the Children's Book Council, and the schools and libraries of Seattle, Washington. It has already "proven that the newest of the mass communications media can be used constructively without loss of interest."[2]

It is impossible to predict the impact that television will have on the library program in the elementary school and on children's reading, but the school librarian can begin immediately to capitalize on what the children see on TV and use it as a means of broadening their interests and reading horizons. She can set up book displays which will supplement the information which they obtain from programs. If there is a TV story hour, she may introduce the book or the author to the children before the program. She may review other books in the library by the same author, set up an exhibit of the author's books, or plan an exhibit of other books about the same subject. She may utilize the sports events programs as a background for a bulletin board display or for an exhibit of sports stories or biographies of famous players. A "TV Corner" on the bulletin board may adjoin the "Radio Corner." Here the librarian may post a list of the best programs for children, giving both channels and hours, and suggest books to read in connection with the programs. There are innumerable ways in which the elementary library can be tied into this new form of communication which is so enticing to children. TV is not to be feared by the school librarian. She must realize that, used intelligently, TV can and does encourage reading. She needs to keep herself well informed about its development and its possibilities for utilization. She needs to show initiative, imagination, and vision in making plans for capitalizing on it as a new and important supplement to the library program.

The library in relation to the reading program

In considering the functions of the elementary school library, one should not overlook the importance of the contribution it makes in providing a basis for the modern reading program. Educators are coming to appreciate the vital relationship which exists between reading skills and reading activities. The reading program is only at its beginning with the instruction of reading techniques. All children must finally acquire for themselves skill in the art of reading through

---

[2] Nancy Faulkner, "Books Versus Boxtops," *Wilson Library Bulletin,* XXVI (June 1952), 811-16. Also Chapter 8 in *The World of Children's Books* (New York: Children's Book Council, 1952).

constant participation in meaningful reading activities. The modern reading program recognizes the necessity of supplying children with something worth while to read as well as instruction in how to read. In order to carry out this function, the elementary school library needs a liberal collection of fine children's books, both fiction and nonfiction, covering a wide range of interests and varying in reading difficulty.

Great strides in the teaching of reading have resulted from the recognition of the individual differences of children in reading capacities, interests, and abilities. The library performs an especially important function in providing materials to meet these individual differences.

The library affords children manifold opportunities to acquire reading experience of all types. It is only through extensive reading that children learn to form their own judgments about books and develop standards of taste and appreciation. The library affords children an opportunity to explore in the book world—to thumb through many books, to taste and sample some, and finally to select and read those which appeal to them.

Another phase of the reading program is the opportunity which the library affords for the informational and reference type of reading. Such fields as science and social studies require this type. The library provides not only the materials necessary for this type of reading but also instruction in the use of books and in library techniques which enables children to carry on such reading activities successfully.

The library—an integrating factor

One of the important problems in the field of elementary education is how to develop a more integrative type of educational experience for elementary school children. Subject matter learned in isolation has little of permanent educational value. The school library has the advantage of serving as an integrating factor in the child's educational experience. In his reading there he is able to pursue his own interests and develop new interests through books and reading. The reading in which he engages is a purposeful activity and represents a real life situation as contrasted with the artificial situation involved in the ordinary reading lesson or classroom assignment. The opportunity to read widely on a given topic helps him to understand that knowledge is not confined to textbooks, and he gains skill in selecting and evaluating information from various sources. The vicarious experiences gained from wide reading in the library produce a profound effect in the expansion of the child's intellectual horizon and his total personality.

The integrating force of the library is not automatic, however. The program must be carefully planned and continually nurtured. This planning and nurturing involves the central school administration, the school library supervisor, if there is one, the principal, the school librarian, and every teacher in the school. The initial planning of the various relationships involved in the integration of library facilities and the curriculum is essentially an administrative matter since it involves the organization of courses of study, policies concerning the selection of books, plans for the use and circulation of library materials, and for the daily use of the library. True integration is the act of bringing all parts together in a whole, and thus the library must be carefully fitted into the curriculum pattern of the school, a pattern which is constantly changing.

Courses of study are constantly being revised, and teacher committees working under some central authority in charge of curriculum usually do the actual work of revision or rewriting. The school librarian often serves on these committees because of the unique contributions she can make to curriculum construction. She is the materials specialist in the school. Her training and her work give her unusual opportunities to know children's books. She has skill in the use of standard book selection aids. She has the ability to locate new materials and to evaluate them in the light of the needs of the courses of study. She is able to give firsthand information on what types of books appeal most to children at the various levels of development. She can suggest books for the accelerated reader, books for the slow reader, story books with factual information, and magazines and pamphlets which will be suitable for use with the various courses of study. She knows the various types of audio-visual aids and the best sources for obtaining them. She specializes in the making of bibliographies for all reading levels and subject interests. The integrating force of the librarian in the building of courses of study is unlimited.

Copies of all courses of study used in the school need to be in the library for the use of the school librarian. She must familiarize herself with the courses in order to build up the book collection so that it has a vital part in the curriculum. She needs this information also in order to serve the reference needs of both teachers and children. In fact, the librarian who is not thoroughly familiar with the courses of study is unable to give the leadership needed for coordinating the library with the total school program.

Often supplementary books in such fields as social studies, science, music, physical education, or the teaching of reading are selected by book committees working under the direction of a special supervisor. Often school librarians are members of these committees. Sometimes they are not. Sometimes the committees recommending books are the same committees that build the courses of study. At any rate, the books selected by these book committees are supplementary books which are essential for the courses of study. They form an important part of the book collection of the library and are circulated to classrooms as needed. They are certainly integrating forces.

The librarian needs to keep in touch with classroom activities by frequent conferences with teachers so that she might suggest suitable materials related to units of work in progress in the classroom. The teacher, too, needs to keep the school librarian advised of classroom work in progress and new activities being planned in order to get the maximum from the library. Close cooperation between teacher and librarian is one of the most important factors in maintaining the integrating role of the library in the school.

Even the technical processes involved in setting up a library according to accepted library standards can be closely integrated with the school program. The librarian can make certain adjustments in the card catalog on the basis of the curriculum, in order to have the catalog bear a direct relationship to the school program. Subject headings assigned to catalog cards may follow closely the subjects or units in such courses of study as science and social studies, since it is in these fields where most reference work is carried on. Pamphlets and pictures may be classified by using subject headings taken from the courses of study.

A planned program for using the library is essential for real integration. Any plan is satisfactory if it makes the library accessible to all children for reference and reading purposes and if it provides time for children to go to the library regularly. Only through careful planning does the library become an integrating factor in the life of the school.

The library—a guidance center

Modern education teaches that it is the function of the school to accept the child at whatever stage of development he may be and to help him grow. The aim is to teach the whole child, and the task involves the cooperation of every teacher and department within the school. The school library may become the school's main laboratory for guidance of individual children. The school librarian is in a strategic position to learn about the child's interests. Through conferences with teachers and through examining scores on the many standard tests which the child is given, she learns of his scholastic standing and his abilities. Through her friendly attitude she learns of his previous experiences both in school and out of school. Through observation, she discovers his status with his classmates and teachers. Through individual conferences, or as he participates in group discussions, she learns of his reactions to various situations he finds in books or to types of characters he reads about.

This understanding of individual children gives the librarian a decided advantage in assisting in the guidance program of the school. She is often the first to discover the "why" of a problem child's behavior pattern and is the first to offer a solution to the problem. The solution often lies in "work." Work in the library offers any child an opportunity for growth. The librarian can assign jobs to children on the basis of their needs, abilities, and interests in such a way that each day brings to them some measure of success in their work. Jobs are many. There are pockets to be pasted in new books; books must be checked to see that there are no pages missing; materials must be stamped with the library stamp of identification; the room needs to be arranged for the story hour; bulletin boards must be planned; there are posters to be made; stories need to be prepared for the story hour in primary grades; books need to be charged out to classrooms or checked in; shelves need straightening. Such diversity of work gives opportunity for all types of children to assume responsibilities. Working in the library becomes a special privilege, and there, side by side, the accelerated child and the retarded child cooperate and share the fun of working with books. Good citizenship is practiced. The accelerated reader increases his book experiences and broadens his outlook. He finds the library an indispensable resource for his inquiring mind. The slow reader gains self-confidence. He discovers that as he succeeds he becomes happier and that the library is a place where he can find easy books about his special interests and interesting jobs that require little reading! Reading guidance, too, gives the librarian a special opportunity to help children with their personal problems. This phase of guidance is discussed fully in Chapter 11, "Reading guidance and library activities."

chapter 3

Organization and administration

of the elementary school library

The functions of the elementary school library were considered in the preceding chapter. In inaugurating and carrying on elementary school library service a school system faces the problem of organizing and administering library service so that these functions may be carried out in an effective way. A successful library program involves the organization of library service in a manner which will facilitate the use of the library by children and teachers. There is little point to having a well-organized library in a school unless the school's program is arranged so that children may make effective use of library resources. This point is stressed because elementary schools sometimes develop quite satisfactory libraries but limit their usefulness through inadequate or ineffective administrative organization. Any satisfactory program of library service involves the whole school program. The library can become an integral part of the learning and living experience of children only in proportion as provision is made for its constant and extensive use.

There are two phases of the administration of elementary school library service. One of these is the administration of library service in the school system as a whole, the other is the administration of library service within the individual school.

ADMINISTRATION OF LIBRARY SERVICE
IN THE SCHOOL SYSTEM

In the administration of elementary school library service in the school system as a whole, there are wide variations of practice in the United States. In some school systems the elementary school library service is administered by the city or county library with the books loaned to the various elementary schools by the city or county library. Under this plan, school library service is usually confined to classroom collections of books, although, in some cases, the books are supplied in a sufficient quantity to be organized in a central library in each large school served. In other school systems, the board of education provides for the maintenance of school library service. The trend toward consolidation of small rural school districts into larger districts has brought about a definite trend toward control of elementary school library service by the board of education. When the board of education maintains library service it is done either by providing a library for each school or by a central distribution system with books circulating from a central book depository or a central library. No matter what the plan, school library service should be the responsibility of the board of education just as other school services are, and both the financial support and educational worth of the school library program should depend upon the board of education.

Whatever the particular plan of operation, it is highly desirable that central administration and supervision be maintained. Efficient library service involves highly specialized training and skills. Book selection, classification, and cataloging, for example, are matters which cannot be trusted to persons without adequate training and preparation. So important is this phase of library service that the board of education of every large city or district where the school system administers elementary school libraries should employ a supervisor, coordinator, or director of libraries who is responsible for the planning and directing of library activities throughout the school system. This type of supervision should be provided also by any county or city library which administers elementary school library service. The person occupying this position should have fine professional training in librarianship in addition to other training and qualifications which make for successful work in educational supervision. The position should have the same status in the school

*Children learn to use
reference aids intelligently.*

*Nonbook materials are
important resources.*

system as other professional supervisory positions, and the supervision, like all educational supervision, should stress leadership rather than inspection. It is advisory and not inspectional. In addition to local supervision many states provide a state supervisor or director of school libraries as part of the state department of education or of the state library.[1] This state leadership has given real impetus to the development of well-planned and adequately financed elementary school libraries and has done much to interpret school library service to the public.

Central supervision of library service

A well-organized plan of central administration includes the following supervisory features:

Expert service and supervision in book selection

Financial economy in quantity purchasing of books and library supplies

Assistance to principals and librarians in organizing and administering individual school libraries

Facilities for pooling experiences and interests in the development of the library program and in the improvement of the total school program

Assistance to principals, teachers, and librarians in developing a total reading program in the school

Guidance to school librarians

Central cataloging which makes for economy and convenience in the mechanical processing of books

Efficient and economical mending and repair service

Uniform standards and practices in libraries throughout the school system

The central library and classroom collections

There are two prevailing conceptions of the manner in which elementary school library service should be organized. One is based on the conception of a central library in each elementary school. The other involves the idea of organizing such service in terms of classroom book collections. It seems unfortunate that these two ideas should be thrown into opposition or juxtaposition. In actual practice, it will be found that there is conflict in the thinking of educators on

---

[1] Ruth Ersted, "School Library Supervisors, National and State," *Library Trends*, I (January 1953), 333-44.

this matter and that a school system often uses one of these plans to the exclusion of the other. The ideal arrangement involves a combination of the two ideas—a central library in each school with provision for the circulation of collections of books to classrooms. Classroom collections alone cannot be regarded as representing in any sense a complete or effective type of library service for an elementary school. Such collections are invariably limited to a relatively small number of books and can never provide a real library experience for children. On the other hand, the central school library which fails to provide for the circulation of book collections to classrooms fails in performing one of its most important functions.

Any plan of library administration which provides for a central library in each school has the following advantages:

It gives children a real library experience which parallels the library situations they will meet in high school, in college, or in the public library. They learn, for example, how books are arranged on library shelves, how to use the card catalog, indexes, reference books, and other resources of the library.

It is financially the most economical plan of administering library service because it avoids unnecessary expenditure for duplication of titles and the heavy expense involved in any plan which requires transportion of books from a source outside the school.

It makes the entire book collection available for the use of the maximum number of children at all times. Book collections permanently located in classrooms are inevitably idle a large portion of the school day.

It provides flexibility in the use of library materials by both children and teachers. It makes a wide selection of materials available to meet the needs of individual children and renders it easy to supply teachers with book collections which really meet classroom needs.

Book circulation from a central depository

Plans of administration which depend upon the distribution of books and library materials from a central depository outside the school have so many disadvantages that they can be recommended only for rural schools or for small schools where it is not feasible to maintain a complete library for each building. Good county or regional library systems which provide library service to rural schools represent this type of service at its best. County or regional library service provides the advantage of central direction and supervision and makes available to each school a much larger number of books and more extensive library services than each school can provide for itself. Furthermore, where a one-, two-, or three-room school attempts to purchase its own book collection, the books are seldom well selected. The collection is necessarily so small that children soon exhaust their interest in it, and the books are not used enough to be worn out and replaced.

In large rural schools, the effectiveness of county library service can be increased by establishing a central library in the school. This enables the school to plan a library program and to enjoy the advantages of a central school library with the book collection provided by the county library. Schools which establish such libraries often find it possible to augment the book collection supplied by the county library with books provided by enthusiastic parent-teacher groups and student groups.

In city systems, plans involving circulation from a library or book depository outside the school are not to be recommended. Such plans are expensive because they always involve trucks and other expensive equipment and additional personnel. They also necessitate a heavy expense for duplicate copies of books. Where the circulation is limited to classroom collections, library service is reduced to the minimum. A collection of fifty or one hundred books for a classroom of thirty or forty pupils cannot provide for much range of individual interest or reading ability. A difficulty which seems inseparable from most plans for this type of circulation is that there is a very annoying lag between need and supply. In a classroom collection of books many children quickly exhaust the books in which they are interested. Sometimes the difficulty is increased by the fact that teachers must go to the central depository to select books or accept fixed collections of books which may bear very little relationship to the reading interests or abilities of their particular classes.

ADMINISTRATION OF LIBRARY SERVICE IN THE INDIVIDUAL SCHOOL

Providing time for using the library

The vitality and success of the library program in any school depends in a large measure on the skill of the principal in developing a type of school organization which provides for the effective use of the library by pupils and teachers. Different principals may accomplish this result in different ways. Any plan is satisfactory which makes the library easily accessible to all children for reference or reading purposes and provides time for children to go to the library regularly. The best plans include a daily allotment of time in the library for each class with provision for individual children and committees of children to use the library at any other time of the day for special work. This arrangement makes it possible to coordinate library and classroom activities effectively. Also the librarian is able to carry on a definite program of activities with each class, which includes instruction in the use of books and libraries, storytelling, group discussions of books and reading, recreational reading, and reading guidance. It is difficult to organize these activities satisfactorily in a school where children come to the library only for reference work or on an indefinite and irregular schedule. Principals who have a high degree of appreciation of the role of the library in the school find no more difficulty in providing regular time for library activities than for arithmetic, spelling, or any other educational activity.

Some principals have opposed the sending of classes to the library on a regular schedule believing that it violates the principle of children's interest. They maintain that children should go to the library only when they are interested in reading or when they have need for reference work. This argument does not appear sound either pedagogically or psychologically. The argument could be applied with equal force to the scheduling of time for any subject or to any organized use of children's time. Few, indeed, are the activities of either children or adults which can be carried on at the exact moment of spontaneous interest. It would seem that there is no more important educational undertaking than for children to learn to budget and use time effectively. Potentially, children always have an interest in books and reading because they are vitally interested in life and living. As a matter of practice, it does not appear that children lose that interest merely because it has to be exercised within reasonable time limits. If further illustration of the point were necessary, one might cite children's enjoyment of swimming, of baseball, or the attendance at a movie, in all of which situations they adjust their interest to the time when they find they can take part in the activity, rather than to that certain moment when it occurs to them they would enjoy it.

In some schools each teacher is left free to determine when and under what circumstances children may go to the library or use library materials. This plan is successful only when teachers are library-minded and are alert to the important place the library might play in the lives of children. Unfortunately many teachers become so absorbed in the ordinary routine of the classroom that they seem to find little time and occasion to devote to the children's interests in books and the library. Even under this plan it becomes necessary to arrange some kind of schedule for the use of the library room in order to avoid conflict between different teachers and classes in their use of the room. While it is possible for a teacher who wishes to take a class to the library to inquire of all other teachers whether or not they are planning to use the library room at a certain period, this is always an inconvenient, inefficient, and irritating situation. A planned schedule is the best solution to this problem.

Circulation of library materials to classrooms

The importance of provision for giving children regular access to the library cannot be overemphasized. Equally important, however, is the necessity of arranging the mechanics for the easy flow of library materials to and from classrooms. Every elementary school library should have an extensive collection of books and materials which are used for the most part in the classrooms. Some of these may be of a type which a teacher may wish to keep in the classroom for the entire duration of a particular unit of work. Other materials she may need only for a period, for a day, or for a week. All supplementary books and materials should be considered a part of the library book collection. Since these materials usually include supplementary readers and other textbooks, it is best to shelve them in a separate section of the library or in the workroom. Long rows of supplementary texts detract from the appearance of the library shelves, and also the special shelving makes for more convenience in moving books in and out of the library. A copy or two of each title useful for reference work may be shelved with the regular library book collection as a convenience to children using the library for reference purposes.

In addition to supplementary books, many other books may be circulated to classrooms. The library should supply all books for the reading tables or library corners in primary classrooms. In the upper grades, classroom circulation is ordinarily limited to books related to classroom activities, while recreational reading is carried on in the library. Classroom circulation must be planned in a manner that will not deplete or weaken the book collection for regular library use.

The system of charging out books to the classroom should be simple and convenient so that teachers do not hesitate to utilize the service because of the red tape involved. Lightweight carrying trays or book trucks enable children to carry conveniently groups of books from the library to classrooms. Without this equipment it is not only inconvenient to move the books back and forth, but they are frequently dropped and damaged in the handling.

The plan and details of the circulation setup and records will naturally depend upon the type of circulation the library maintains. If books are circulated to classrooms only, the book cards signed by the teacher may be kept in a file under the teacher's name. Names may be listed alphabetically in the file as an aid to rapid filing. If books circulate for home use, it seems best to file the book cards, signed by the pupils, under the date the book is due. This enables the librarian to know when books are overdue. No matter what system is set up to keep such records, it must be a simple system which can be easily used by children. There is no place for fines for overdue books in an elementary school, and if a proper library morale is developed most children will be alert to returning materials for the use of others. The librarian must try to see that teachers and pupils alike aid in keeping the collection available for all to use through the prompt return of unused materials. There can be no hard and fast rules concerning the length of time for circulation. Each school will set up its own program depending upon its needs, and the librarian will have to make many, many exceptions to any rules or regulations concerning the use of books. Her main idea is to get materials to teachers and pupils when and for as long as they are needed and to get them back into the library when they are no longer being used. An unused book on a shelf in a classroom may be the very book that some child is seeking in the library.

The library and the curriculum

The type of educational program maintained in an elementary school has a most important bearing on the character and extent of the library service. The planning of the various relationships involved in the coordination of library facilities and the curriculum is essentially an administrative matter since it involves policies of purchasing books, plans for the use and circulation of library materials, and the organization of courses of study in a manner which will facilitate the use of library facilities by children and teachers. In schools following the traditional subject matter program, where teaching is based for the most part on a textbook with perhaps one or two supplementary books, there is little occasion for the use of library materials. In the more creative and dynamic elementary school programs which are now becoming widely developed, extensive use of library materials becomes an absolute necessity.

In school systems where there is close connection between the curriculum and the library, the library collection is developed and planned in the light of curriculum needs. Reference books, supplementary books, audio-visual materials, periodicals, and pamphlet materials are purchased and organized specifically to meet classroom needs. Many courses of study are now organized so that they require the extensive use of library resources, and include in the course of study bibliographies related to each unit of work. Frequently these "unit bibliographies" include page references in specific books and give suggestions for the use of related library materials. The materials listed in the unit bibliographies include various levels of reading in order to take care of the individual reading capacities in any class.

Including library references in courses of study is one of the most effective ways of assuring a close connection between the library and the curriculum. Where extensive use is made of library materials, it becomes important to include such references in courses of study as a means of saving time for both teachers and children. While it might appear that this procedure would deprive children of needed opportunity to do reference work, it will be found in practice that this is not the case. In pursuing particular phases of topics under discussion there will still be many references which can never be placed in a bibliography and which children will need to look up for themselves. The following example from a recent course of study in social studies illustrates the way in which such bibliographies are organized:

ELEMENTARY SOCIAL STUDIES—FOURTH GRADE[2]

Bibliography[3]

Unit III. How California Came to Have Its Spanish Culture

A. Early Explorers

Cameron	El Pueblo
	Cabrillo, 29-35
	Viscaino, 37-41
	Portola, 43-45
Corwin	The Pioneer's Pathway
	Viscaino, 36-40
Dawson	California, The Story of Our Southwest Corner
	Discovery of California, 32-48
Flower	A Child's History of California
	Cabrillo, 26-31
	Drake, 32-36
	Father Serra, 42-47
	Viscaino, 37-41
	Portola, 48-54
Richards	Early California
	Cabrillo, 98-101
	Drake, 102-106
	Viscaino, 113-115
	Portola, 125-142
	Father Serra, 125-142

B. Spanish Settlements in California

Flower	A Child's History of California
	Missions, 55-65
	Presidios, 66
	Pueblos, 66-67
	Ranchos, 75-82

---

[2] Sacramento City Unified School District, *Course in Social Studies for Fourth Grade* (Sacramento, Calif.: Sacramento City Unified School District, September 10, 1951).

[3] Full bibliographic information for each title will be found in the General Bibliography of this course of study.

Heard	Stories of American Explorers and Settlers
	Missions, 67-72

Snedden	Docas, the Indian Boy
	Missions, 57-114
	Ranchos, 121-156

C. Spanish Influence Today

Flower	A Child's History of California
	Spanish names, 181-182
	Spanish customs, 80-82

Hoffman	California Beginnings
	Spanish names, 269-276

Visual Aids

Sound Films	Mission Life
	California Missions
	Rancho Life

Filmstrips	California History
	Sir Francis Drake
	Story of California Missions

Lantern Slides	California Missions

The teacher cooperating with the library

A key person in the functioning of the elementary school library program is the classroom teacher. The attitude of the teacher toward the library is immediately reflected in her methods of teaching and in the attitude of her class. A teacher who has keen appreciation of the part the library may play in the lives of children and in the conduct of the educational program will find constant occasions for the use of the library. The teacher who has little appreciation of the library or its possibilities will naturally make only the most meager use of its resources.

There are many ways in which the classroom teacher can cooperate actively in the development of the elementary school library program. The classroom must always provide the real basis for the functional use of the library. The greatest service the teacher can render is to provide the kind of learning situations which call for the constant use of library facilities. These situations involve such things as the gathering of information for reports, the need to use the card catalog, atlases, dictionaries, and encyclopedias, and the use of the library for the development of hobbies and leisure reading. The teacher, too, can do much to create and develop on the part of children an intelligent interest in the library and its services. This may be done not only by carrying on the type of classroom work which involves the need to use the library but also by frequent discussions of the library and its services. These discussions should include the public library as well as the school library in order that children may be familiar with all of the library resources which are available for their use. Such discussions should not be "scheduled" or "staged" in a formal manner but should come about naturally from classroom situations in which children need to know the answers to such questions as—

> *Where can I get a book about postage stamps?*
> *Where should I look to find the population of Brazil?*
> *Where can I find reproductions of some of the great art master-*
> *   pieces?*
> *How did the people dress in Colonial days?*
> *What kind of leaf is this?*

The classroom teacher can cooperate directly with the school library by furnishing the librarian with lists of books and materials which are needed for classroom activities and by keeping the librarian informed of new activities which are contemplated so that the librarian may have time to organize suitable materials. It is helpful, also, for the teacher to visit the library frequently and confer with the librarian on special classroom activities. This gives the teacher the opportunity to indicate what is needed for her work and gives the librarian the opportunity to offer suggestions as to materials which might be useful. The teacher who is library-minded will find many ways of keeping the work of the classroom in constant touch with the library and of cooperating actively with the librarian in all phases of library activity.

There will be frequent opportunities for the classroom teacher to discuss books informally with children. However, to do this successfully, the teacher must be familiar with the library collection and should read many of the children's books so that she may be regarded by the children as a dependable adviser on books. There will be many occasions to discuss desirable library habits and conduct, including the proper use and care of library books and materials. Finally, the teacher may contribute much to the efficiency of the library by cooperating actively in the care and circulation of library materials, by seeing that library books are properly handled in the classroom as well as in the library, by calling attention to torn pages or loose plates, and, above all, by returning materials to the library when they are due or before they are due, if they are no longer needed.

The librarian cooperating with the classroom

Just as it is a responsibility of the classroom teacher to bring the classroom and its work into the library, so it is the part of the librarian to take the library and its resources into the classrooms. Through tact, sympathy, initiative, patience, and much common sense the librarian must seek to win the wholehearted respect and admiration of the teachers. A friendly disposition on the part of the librarian will aid in creating a friendly attitude toward the library and its program.

The following are suggested as ways in which the librarian may aid in the development of cooperative relationships between the library and the classroom:

Advise with teachers about classroom activities and about reading needs of individual children.

Become familiar with individual children's reading abilities as reflected through standard tests.

Advise teachers of new books and audio-visual materials in which they might be interested through personal conferences and by issuing lists of new materials received.

Advise teachers of interesting and timely magazine articles, pamphlet and picture materials.

Furnish classrooms with lists of books and materials related to displays on classroom bulletin boards. These may be about special holidays, animals, current events, etc. The lists may be accompanied by displays of pictures, book jackets, and books.

Fill orders promptly for materials for use in the classroom so that classroom work is not delayed.

Keep in touch with the progress of classwork by frequent conferences with teachers.

Make suggestions of suitable stories, films, and records related to units of work in progress in the classroom.

Set up in the library special troughs, shelves, or displays of books for the use of particular classes.

Visit classrooms in order to be in close touch with the educational program.

Seek the advice of teachers and children when ordering new books for the library.

Ask the principal to devote at least one faculty meeting each year to a discussion of the library and its services.

Advise with teacher-leaders of special groups, such as Boy Scouts, Girl Scouts, Camp Fire Girls, stamp clubs, science clubs, or other school groups, in order to fit the library into their programs.

Pupil assistants and library clubs

No matter how small the library there are many time-consuming tasks involved in the operation of it. Children can assume many of these tasks and thus share in the management of the library. Pupil assistants are a necessity. The librarian will want to select her assistants carefully. She may wish to confer with the teachers and principal about certain children. Pupil assistants may include the gifted child, the average child, and the retarded child, for the tasks are many and the knowledge on the part of the children that what they do is an important school service brings personal satisfaction to all. (*See* "The library—a guidance center," p.13.) The group may be called by an appropriate name such as "The Book Worms," "Book Bees," "Library Club," or "Library Service Club." By its accomplishments it gains prestige, and membership in the group becomes a real honor. If the group is large the librarian may divide it into various committees thus utilizing the skills of individual children. Committee work needs to be carefully planned and directed. A "Service Committee" may have as its function the opening and processing of new materials, plus service at the charging desk. A "Decoration or Room Committee" may be in charge of planning bulletin boards and exhibits. A "Publicity Committee" may arrange library displays on hall bulletin boards, tell stories to primary grades, advertise new books to classrooms, and prepare news items for the school or local newspaper. A "Visual-Aids Committee" may assist with the circulation of visual-aids materials and also operate the projection machines. The "club" needs to have regular "business" meetings with the librarian for discussion of problems and for evaluation of work, and at least one social meeting during the year for fun. It is the logical group to assist with Book Week plans and to act as hosts whenever meetings are held in the library. A well-organized library club, working under the supervision of a librarian with imagination, can become a source of real inspiration to all members—the gifted, the retarded, and the average child.

chapter 4

Elementary school
library personnel

A library is more than a room filled with books. It is distinctly a functioning and service organization. In fact the services which are rendered constitute the only reason for its existence. No matter how ample or attractive the library room or how adequate the book collection, a library is only as effective as the personnel in charge.

The question of elementary school library personnel might be considered from either an idealistic and theoretical point of view or from a distinctly realistic and practical point of view. Ideally we would like to think of every elementary school library as being in charge of a librarian who has adequate professional training, wide familiarity with the modern elementary school program and teaching methods, and with the fortunate qualities of personality which make for the happiest working relationships with children and teachers. However, if this discussion is to be generally valuable as a contribution to the elementary school library program, it must face the problems of personnel in a practical and realistic manner. Of all the elementary school libraries in operation in the United States today, only a very small percentage are under the charge of persons having adequate professional training as children's librarians. Many are under the charge of persons having some professional library training, and many, especially in small elementary schools, are under the charge of teachers and others having no professional library training.

The point of view here presented is that the elementary school library program is in a state of evolution and that it will be a good many years before we may hope to see all libraries under the charge of full-time professionally trained personnel. But during this period of evolution, school systems may do much to give direction and speed to the process of improving the personnel in charge of elementary school libraries. Another viewpoint underlying the entire discussion of this problem of personnel is that it involves something more than mere professional training. Not all persons who are able to secure library credentials have the characteristics and personal qualifications which make for success in the elementary school library field.

It is the purpose of this chapter to analyze the functions and qualifications of the elementary school librarian and to consider the various types of library personnel which may, as a matter of practice, have charge of elementary school library service.

Functions of the school librarian

The first obvious function of the school librarian is to have charge of the school library, the organization and use of the book collection, and the general organization of library service to children and teachers. In most school systems this includes the cataloging and classifying of books, although in some large cities these technical processes are handled centrally for all school libraries within the city.

The librarian shares a part of the responsibility for seeing that the library constantly functions as an integral part of the school and not as a separate and independent unit. This responsibility involves the principal and the teachers as well. But the librarian is always the key person in carrying out the processes involved in maintaining the library as a cooperative part of the school. This integration of the library with the school program is not accomplished in mysterious or abstract ways but comes about as the result of definite plans and organization. It results, for example, from such activities on the part of the librarian as building up and making available to pupils and teachers a well-rounded collection of library materials which meets the needs of the classroom for both curricular and recreational materials. A librarian who is alert to the needs of children and teachers is not likely to have great difficulty in making the library an integral part of the school.

In order to keep the library in step with the changing curriculum, it becomes a function of the librarian to familiarize herself with the entire elementary school program, to understand its underlying philosophies, and to be alert to changes in materials or methods which are coming about in the elementary field. It is only through this understanding that the librarian can assist teachers or pupils effectively with their classwork and appreciate their problems and needs for library materials.

Another function of the school librarian is to supplement the work of the classroom teacher by stimulating and encouraging interest in recreational reading and by giving reading guidance to children.

It is the school librarian who must develop the atmosphere and services of the library in such a way that the library will become a place which students and faculty will enjoy using because of its pleasing and friendly atmosphere. This is particularly important in the elementary school where children are getting their first extensive experience with the library. An atmosphere of cold, sepulchral silence can do as much to render a library ineffective as an inadequate or uninteresting book collection. The library should be an easy place to use. It should be a place where children do not always have to walk on tiptoe and speak in whispers. Its general atmosphere should be such that the child will remember with pleasure his moments spent there. This atmosphere is attained, not by rules and regulations, but by constant stress on the type of good citizenship which is based on a respect for the rights of others. It comes from everyday living with people who observe these rights and expect others as a matter of course to do the same. In this sense the librarian may become one of the best teachers of citizenship and social behavior in the entire school.

Professional training and mental qualifications

The elementary school librarian should have adequate professional library training. While it does not come within the scope of this book to discuss in detail the library courses involved, it may be stated that one year's training in a good library school should afford the necessary training. This would assume, however, that the emphasis during the year should be on school libraries. The training should include courses in children's literature, book selection, organization and administration of the school library, storytelling, reference, cataloging, and classification.

In addition to professional library training, the elementary school librarian should have good, basic, teacher training for the elementary field. In many states this is covered by the general requirement of certification for all persons employed in the elementary school field. The elementary school librarian should have a broad knowledge of the various fields of subject matter in the elementary school and a good cultural background which gives meaning and significance to the entire educational process. She should have a wide knowledge of children's books gained through study and extensive reading of children's books and she must study the children and their interests continually in order to know their reading abilities and tastes. Children soon become suspicious of the librarian who recommends books only from hearsay, and they have vast respect for the librarian who knows many books and is able to select good ones. Courses in children's literature and child psychology are not enough. The effective school librarian must continue to read widely in the field of children's literature. She must be well grounded in the field of child psychology in order to deal effectively with children and must continue to study each child as a unique personality. The librarian must have a thorough knowledge of reference books related to elementary school work so that she can assist children effectively in using them.

The librarian must be familiar with modern classroom methods. Since methods of teaching change, the librarian can keep step with the classroom only through constant study of the changing elementary field. The librarian must know how materials are to be used in the classroom in order to know how to relate the work of the library to the needs of the classroom. She needs an intelligent understanding of the principles of education and school administration in order to manage the library in keeping with good principles of educational administration. Her knowledge of technical processes involved in school library work must be so thorough that she can organize and manage a school library and do the necessary technical work of processing, handling, and caring for books and other library materials without confusion or noticeable effort.

In order to succeed in a high degree, an elementary school librarian must have the ability to handle children so that the maintenance of order and of discipline do not present a problem. Some persons with very adequate professional training never make effective elementary school librarians because of this basic lack of ability and capacity for handling groups of children effectively. A good librarian needs the same ability to manage and direct children that the good classroom teacher has.

Personal qualifications

It has been suggested that mere professional training alone will not produce an effective school librarian. School superintendents and principals in interviewing candidates for library positions should give particular attention to certain matters of personality which become the keynote of the librarian's success. The matters of personality referred to are not entirely abstract or subjective qualities. Many of them are, in fact, definitely objective and are easily recognized.

Probably the most basic personal qualification should be a genuine and sincere enthusiasm for books and life. A person who does not love books is not an asset in the library. Children very quickly detect shallow sentimentalities, frenzied enthusiasm, and insincere attitudes. A librarian who reads and knows books and has sound standards of judgment is in a fair position to deal with children in their relationships to books.

Another important personal qualification is a genuine liking for children and a sympathetic understanding of them and their problems. Fortunate is the librarian who regards her task as introducing children to books rather than introducing books to children. And in proportion as she likes and understands children, she is likely to prove successful.

A qualification of great value is breadth of interest achieved through study, reading, participation in a wide variety of activities, and travel. Children respond to richness of personality and, like adults, are not inspired by persons who are nonentities. The librarian with broad interests has little difficulty in gaining the respect and interest of the children.

The librarian's physical health and characteristics also have a very important bearing on her success. Vitality and good health are basic.

From these emanate a whole train of desirable qualities, such as physical poise, mental poise, good humor, self-reliance, and personal magnetism. All of these are valuable qualifications in dealing with children.

Allied with the matter of vitality and good health is the matter of personal appearance. This fortunately is a phase of personality about which all persons may do a great deal. The librarian can dress attractively and neatly. She can exercise care in personal grooming. She can avoid peculiar and annoying mannerisms, and, in a large measure, she can cultivate the qualities of voice and manner which make for pleasant social relationships. It is possible to cultivate also the social qualities which are necessary for effectiveness in a position which is highly cooperative in its nature. Such social qualities include consideration and thoughtfulness of others, avoidance of gossip and comments relative to associates, ability to listen thoughtfully to others, and a serenity of manner and voice which may serve to allay irritations in working with others.

TYPES OF SCHOOL LIBRARY PERSONNEL

While the discussion of library personnel might be limited only to elementary school librarians with adequate professional training, a realistic view of the problem seems to make it desirable to consider all types of library personnel which, as a matter of practice, will be found in elementary school libraries. The discussion here presented is addressed particularly to superintendents and principals who will be employing and assigning personnel to libraries.

The full-time, trained librarian

If the elementary school is large enough or school finances permit, the desirable practice always would be the selection of a full-time, trained librarian possessing the desirable personal characteristics for effective work in the elementary school. This would mean a librarian especially trained for children's library work rather than for general library work. She should also have a background of training or experience which would assure an understanding of the elementary educational program, and should possess the characteristics and instincts of the successful elementary school teacher. Many persons who might succeed well in a high school or college library do not have the characteristics which make for success in an elementary school. It is distinctly a mistake to assign to elementary school library work persons who have only generalized library training or persons who have not been successful in public library or high school library work and are seeking a position in an elementary school library on the theory that "it is easier" in the elementary school. An effective elementary school librarian is not likely to develop from a person who has been a failure in other library work.

The teacher-librarian

Many small schools and many school systems which are beginning the development of elementary school libraries find it imperative to use teacher-librarians; that is, persons who teach part of the day and have charge of the library part of the day. The degree of effectiveness of this plan depends on the quality of the teacher and the extent of her training in library work. Many school systems have developed this plan so that it is yielding excellent results because the teachers have taken occasion to acquire professional library training which is necessary to make this type of arrangement successful.

Under the best circumstances, this arrangement has some distinct advantages. It makes it possible for a small school to maintain a well-organized library under the direction of a person who has sufficient library training to carry on the work effectively. The teacher-librarian has the advantage, not enjoyed by the full-time librarian, of being in active daily contact with the curriculum and classroom teaching problems. She is, therefore, able to sense and appreciate the types of library service needed to coordinate library efforts effectively with classroom needs.

There are some disadvantages which may be encountered in the plan of using teacher-librarians. Superintendents and principals may assign to the library teachers who are not qualified either by training or by temperament to handle the work successfully. Teachers assigned to the library may fail to develop on the job and secure the professional library training they need. Sometimes older teachers are assigned to the library on the theory that library work is easier than classroom work, and they may have little interest in further professional growth and no imagination for the job. The greatest disadvantage, however, is that the teacher-librarian often has too much work to do. The handling of a library involves a vast amount of daily work in the processing of books, circulation of books, keeping of records, decoration of the library room, organizing of classroom collections for teachers, and other details necessary in the carrying out of library routines. In addition to this work, the librarian may have full responsibility for teaching a class. Principals should be aware of this heavy load and should seek every opportunity to relieve the teacher-librarian of additional responsibilities.

As in the selection of full-time librarians, the superintendent or principal needs to exercise the greatest care in selecting teacher-librarians. The same qualities which have been described for a good elementary school librarian are completely applicable to the teacher-librarian. Once a teacher is assigned responsibility for the library, her working day should be so arranged that she actually has part of the day assigned to library work rather than having to carry this obligation on top of a full teaching day. And there should be the clearly understood obligation on the part of the teacher assigned to the library to have, or to acquire, the necessary basic professional training in library work to handle the assignment effectively.

The teacher as librarian

In small schools and in school systems with very limited budgets, if the school is to have a library at all, it may be necessary to assign the work of the library to some teacher who has no library training. The school in this situation faces one of two alternatives: either to attempt nothing in the way of library service, or to begin in a very limited way by placing one of the teachers in charge of the library. While this practice cannot be recommended generally, it is vastly better than having no library and no central book service. In selecting a teacher for this special work, the superintendent or principal should have in mind the kind of qualifications which make for success. The teacher selected should have a definite interest in books and should be an outstanding classroom teacher. The work requires that she possess well-established habits of orderliness and system. She needs the ability to cooperate with other teachers and with children of different ages. She should be young enough in spirit to be adaptable to new ideas—potentially the same characteristics which have been described for the ideal elementary school librarian.

Some schools have established the practice of assigning each teacher to act as librarian for her own class. This arrangement has many disadvantages and is never to be recommended. In this scheme, no one person is responsible for a continued program of library activities. No one is responsible for the library room, its arrangement, decorations, and general upkeep. The technical details of book ordering, of cataloging and classification, and of general library organization can never be handled efficiently under this plan because this work requires technical training which teachers do not have. Not every teacher can be considered an authority on children's books and reading, and few are qualified to give expert guidance in reading. All library activities will vary according to the interests and abilities of individual teachers. Since no one is definitely responsible for the library, it is far better to assign the library to one teacher even though she may have no library training. "What is everybody's business may become nobody's business" with the result that the school library cannot take its rightful place in the life of the school.

Other personnel in charge of the library

While it is recognized that some schools make a practice of placing the library in charge of vice-principals, clerks, students, parents, custodians, and others, none of these practices can be commended as desirable even in emergency situations. The purpose of the library is to render service. Practically never do people of the type mentioned have the training or ability to render effective service. The maintenance, operation, and services of any worth-while library require accurate and definite knowledge regarding the processing, shelving, and handling of books. Seldom is this type of help capable of doing even a fair job in this direction. Probably the most important function of the school librarian is to guide and assist children with their educational problems and their recreational reading. Almost never are persons of the groups mentioned able to aid children well in these activities.

The most important single requisite for effective library service is the librarian herself. Regardless of the particular type of personnel in charge—that is, whether full-time librarian, teacher-librarian, or teacher—the librarian must have a vision of the role which the library has to play in the modern elementary school, and she must have professional training and the personality to translate this vision into reality. Because her role is a dual one, she should show recognition of the dual character of her work by maintaining her professional standing and status both as a teacher and as a librarian.

Supervisor or director of school libraries

As suggested in the chapter on organization and administration, central supervision is an essential phase of elementary school library service, supervision which stresses leadership rather than inspection. In any situation which involves a large number of school libraries, there should be a supervisor or director of school libraries. Because of the nature of the service, this is always an important position and the person holding it should be thoroughly qualified for the position. Since the work involves the supervision of library service in all its aspects, the first qualification of the supervisor should be thorough professional library training. This library training should at least equal in amount the training of any library personnel which is to be supervised.

In addition to professional library training, the supervisor should have the training in the educational field and the personal qualities which are essential to the success of any educational supervisor. Good basic training in the educational field is necessary because school library service is essentially an educational service. It is especially important that the library supervisor should continue to study and grow in both the library and the educational fields in order that the library service may keep abreast of new developments in education. Library supervision requires good administrative and organizing ability in order to handle the many problems in these fields. The nature of the position requires the personal qualifications which are necessary in dealing successfully with people. Among such desirable qualifications are good judgment, poise, breadth of vision, courtesy, cooperativeness, consideration for others, ability to give and receive criticism gracefully, ability to present ideas effectively in both written and oral form, personal culture, and enthusiasm.

SCHOOL LIBRARY PERSONNEL AND THE LIBRARY PROFESSION

Any person who serves in a school library needs to become familiar with educational and professional library organizations. Where possible, membership should be maintained in these important groups. It is through cooperation and combination of effort that organizations become potent forces in any profession. School librarians need the publications and services of their organizations and every organization needs the wholehearted support of members of the profession. The leading organizations and coordinating agencies are listed below.

ASSOCIATIONS

American Library Association, 50 East Huron St., Chicago 11, Ill. The national association of librarians. Membership dues are based on salary of the librarian. Dues include subscription to the *A.L.A. Bulletin*. School librarians are organized within the A.L.A. in a division known as the American Association of School Librarians. For school librarians membership in this division can be requested with membership in the A.L.A. without payment of additional dues.

National Education Association, 1201 16th St., N. W., Washington, D. C. The national association of members of the teaching profession. Membership dues include the *N.E.A. Journal*.

State Library Association. The association on the state level for promoting the library profession. Many have sections for school librarians.

State School Library Association. Several states have an organization for school librarians which is separate from both the state library association and the state education association. Some of these associations publish fine bulletins and are very active groups.

State Education Association. The state association for members of the teaching profession. Many have sections for school librarians.

AGENCIES

United States Office of Education, Washington, D. C. A national government agency for the promotion of education in all fields and levels. There is a Specialist in School Libraries, in the Division of Library Service.

State Department of Education. The state agency for the promotion of public schools. Some states have a school library supervisor or director on the staff.

State Library Agency. The official agency for the promotion of libraries. Some agencies have a school library supervisor or director on the staff.

chapter 5

The physical setup
of the library

S chool library service cannot be evaluated in terms of the physical setup and yet the manner in which the library is housed, furnished, and equipped can aid materially in providing more efficient service. When new elementary school buildings are being planned, the principal and librarian should confer with the architect in planning the school library quarters. The architect must have a thorough understanding of the purposes of the school library and of the activities that will take place in it before he begins his work. The library must be functionally designed to meet the needs of the group it is to serve. Floor plans must include a consideration of the furniture and equipment to be accommodated. It is not unusual to find good furniture and equipment so crowded into a small room that much of its value is lost.

The American Library Association has recently released a 98-frame, 35-millimeter filmstrip in color entitled *School Library Quarters,* produced by Virginia McJenkin and Kathleen Moon of the Fulton County School System in Georgia. It shows details of shelving for both book and nonbook materials; furniture; wall, floor, and window treatment; workrooms and audio-visual facilities; reading room areas; storage spaces; and effective uses of color. The price of the filmstrip is $15. It has much to offer anyone planning school library facilities.

The following pamphlets are highly recommended to both principals and architects:

American Association of School Librarians. Committee on Planning School Library Quarters. *Dear Mr. Architect.* 2d ed. Chicago: American Library Association, 1952. 50c.

> Completely rewritten. Practical suggestions to architects in planning efficient school libraries. Covers essential service and work areas, furnishings, and equipment minimums. Includes photographs of actual school libraries, as well as numerous diagrams of recommended layouts and equipment. Bibliography.

Illinois Library Association. Sub-Committee on Library Service to Schools Planning Board. *Planning School Library Quarters.* Chicago: American Library Association, 1950. $1.50.

> Considers the place and function of the school library. Discusses location of the library within the building, lighting, decoration, layout, furniture, and equipment for housing all types of materials. Good pictures, floor plans, and suggested lists of minimum equipment.

American Library Association. *School Libraries for Today and Tomorrow: Functions and Standards.* Chicago: The Association, 1945. $1.

> Standards officially adopted by the A.L.A. Council. Discusses services of the school library, standards for personnel, book collection and other resources, housing, financing, administration, and supervision. Selected bibliography.

Location of the library

Convenience in use requires that the library be centrally located in the building. The meaning of the term *centrally located* will vary considerably in different building situations. However, certain generalizations can be made with regard to location of the library. It is desirable to have the library near the classes which will make the most use of it. For example, children in the intermediate and upper grades will use the library for reference purposes much more than children in the primary grades. They will in all probability make more use of the room for all their library activities than will the primary grades. For this reason it is logical to place the library in the intermediate and upper-grade section of the school, rather than in the primary section. Such a location may make distances greater between the library and primary classrooms, yet the location will provide more convenient access for the teachers and children who make the most constant use of library facilities. It may be desirable to have the room near the main entrance to the building or the administrative offices as a convenience to teachers and children in checking out and returning books. The room should always be away from the noise of the playground, gymnasium, and the music room, even though this may mean sacrificing a more central location. The location should be such that the library will be a light, sunny, airy room with plenty of window space.

Capacity of the library quarters

The size and capacity of the library quarters will be determined by the school enrollment, the size of the anticipated book collection, the type of school program, and in many cases by the space available in the school for library use. In a building where library facilities can be provided only by converting existing classrooms into a library, what can be accomplished is determined by the space which is available. If only an ordinary classroom is available, it can be planned to accommodate about forty pupils. The cloakroom can be converted into a small workroom. Adequate space can often be provided by removing or altering the partition between adjoining classrooms. Removing the partition between the two cloakrooms will usually provide sufficient space for a convenient workroom and for shelves for the housing of supplementary textbooks. If library quarters are being planned in a new building, they should be planned in anticipation of the future growth of the school.

In any school, the library quarters should be large enough to take care of regularly assigned classes plus additional pupils who may need to use the library for special work, and should be of ample size to provide for the services which are expected to be rendered in the school.

The library workroom

A workroom for the use of the librarian is a necessity. The librarian must have some place where she can process new books, where she can mount pictures and pamphlet materials, and where she can lay out and plan displays and exhibits. She needs space to keep library supplies in an orderly manner, space for large colored paper used for mountings, and space to house flower vases and bowls when not in use. The librarian needs a place and space in which she can spread out her working materials and leave them where they will be undisturbed until she can get time to finish her plans.

The workroom should always adjoin the library for convenience. It must be carefully and wisely planned for its functional purpose. It should contain regulation bookshelves to house new books during the processing period and to house books which are removed from circulation awaiting repair. It should be provided with a sink and running water and with electric outlets. There should be space to spread out books while they are being processed and to mount pictures. Such space can be provided by the addition of a long drainboard to the sink, by a wide shelf attached to the wall which can be lowered flat against the wall when not in use, or merely by the addition of a long table. In a small workroom the drainboard or shelf is most practical since the room may be too small to take care of a large table.

Cupboard space should be designed for the materials which are to be housed. Doors on cupboards will prevent the accumulation of dust on materials which are used only occasionally. Large shallow drawers may be placed under the drainboard or in the cupboard to house large posters, flat maps, and large colored papers used for bulletin board displays or mountings. A practical size for these drawers is from 30 to 40 inches in width, 30 inches from front to back and 2 to 3 inches in depth. The actual size will depend upon the size of materials to be accommodated. The room should have a window to insure air and light and should also have artificial light, if necessary, to provide ample light. When an ordinary classroom is converted into a library, the cloakroom can often be converted into a suitable workroom.

A committee room

The success of a modern elementary school program which includes classroom activities depends greatly upon the physical facilities of the library. Committees of children working on special topics need to come to the library for reference work. This type of work may require that the children discuss their problems, lay plans for each individual's contribution to the work, bring together their findings as a group, and finally make up a cooperative report. All such work necessitates more or less conversation, and, although the talking is the "hum of work," it may prove disturbing to other children who may be reading or it may conflict with the library activities of a class in the library. For this reason it is highly desirable to have a small "committee room" adjoining the library. The supervision of this room can be simplified by the use of glass partitions so that any work carried on in the room is under the observation of the librarian. In a small school which is unable to provide a committee room, a secluded corner of the library may be set aside for the special use of committees or groups.

Preview or "listening" room

If the library becomes the center for all types of audio-visual aids, it is only logical that a room for previewing films and listening to radio programs and recordings should adjoin the library or be located near it. The size of the room will depend upon how it is to be used, but regardless of size it will need to be soundproof and provided with proper shelving and other space units for housing movie projectors, slide projectors, phonographs, screens, and other equipment. It will also need special electric outlets for use with projectors and phonographs.

Walls, floors, and ceilings

While most of the wall space will be used for shelving, a prominent section should be reserved for a bulletin board. This bulletin board should be at least 3 feet by 10 feet, should be so placed that it commands interest and attention, and should be at the eye level of the children. Small sections of wall space which are not desirable for shelving may be used for bulletin boards, thus adding to the general attractiveness of the room. The library floors should always be covered. Satisfactory floor coverings include cork tile, linotile, linoleum, or asphalt tile. These materials are available in many attractive, plain colors. The ceilings should be acoustically treated.

Lighting

Lighting should be carefully planned. Because the library is ordinarily a large room, it is usually necessary to provide artificial lighting. The lighting should be adequate to provide 20- to 35-foot candlepower on any table in the room. The best type of light fixture is the indirect or semi-indirect ceiling fixture. Fluorescent lighting has proved satisfactory. The colors used in walls and ceilings have an important effect on the lighting. Light buff, light gray, or white tones, with sea green or light blue, are good colors for walls. Ivory white is a good color for the ceiling.

Shelving

The long lengths of wall space in the library should be used for shelving. Electric light switches, thermostats, and radiators should be placed so as not to interfere with wall space needed for shelves. All library shelving should conform to established standards. Shelves which are too long sag with the weight of books. Shelves which are too deep make it difficult to shelve books properly. Shelves which are too high are impractical and inconvenient for children. Shelving may be either fixed or adjustable. Adjustable shelving is slightly more expensive, but has the advantage of being adaptable to re-arrangement of the book collection. If adjustable shelving is used, it must be constructed so that shelves are secure and do not tilt or collapse under the weight of books.

The following are standards for elementary school library shelving:

Length of shelf between partitions—3 feet.
Width (depth) of shelf—8 inches.
Thickness of shelf—¾ to 1 inch.
Space in the clear between shelves—bottom shelf 12 inches, other shelves 10 inches.
Height of shelving—5 shelves.
All shelves should be built plain with no overhanging trim either at the top or between shelves. Any overhanging trim interferes with the handling of books.
Mop board below lower shelf—6 inches.

All shelving should be open. Doors interfere with easy access to books. If fixed shelving is used, the bottom shelf of each section of books should be built with 12 inches in the clear between it and the next shelf to provide for oversize books which need to be housed in that section. Also, it is a good plan to build one entire section with 12 inches in the clear between shelves to take care of large reference books such as encyclopedias.

Many books for children do not conform to conventional sizes for books. These odd sizes are not always picture books but include books on all subjects and on all grade levels. Even if adjustable shelving is used, special shelves for these oversize books are essential. Where space is ample, a series of wide, sloping shelves may be used, although this arrangement will not house many books. A special rack built with a sloping shelf on the top and high, narrow sections of shelves underneath is excellent. The shelf underneath should be about 15 inches high and 14 inches deep, with plywood upright partitions at 9-inch intervals. It may be built as a movable rack or as a part of the permanent shelving. This type of rack houses many books in a small space and adds to the attractiveness of the library by displaying books in an interesting manner. Sometimes it is possible to fit a rack of this type under the windows in the room. The top shelf may be left flat, thus providing a fine space for exhibits or plants. Another plan is to build this type of shelving under a recessed bulletin board or to adapt the two lower shelves of the regular shelving for it. Plans for the housing of oversize books must be carefully worked out at the time the library is being planned.

Suggested standards for furniture and equipment

Library equipment should follow well-defined standards. For this reason it is best to purchase library equipment from a reliable firm dealing in library furniture. Some schools cannot afford to purchase adequate library equipment. The equipment may have to be built in the school manual-training shop or in a local cabinet shop. If the equipment is made locally, the greatest care should be exercised to have it conform to library standards.

Tables and chairs. Either tables and chairs or individual desks may be used for library seating. Tables and chairs are recommended because they give a more informal atmosphere. Individual desks tend to formalize the library both in appearance and in fact. The tables may be either rectangular or circular, seating not more than six pupils. Rectangular tables have the advantage of being more easily placed in the ordinary library room. Tables should be of different heights in order to seat children of different sizes comfortably. The standard table for adults is 30 inches high. This is too high for elementary school children. The heights of elementary school library tables should be 24 inches, 26 inches, and 28 inches, the number of each size depending on the grades that will use the room. The 26-inch height table is the average height, and there should probably be as many of this size as of the two other sizes combined.

Library chairs need to be chosen carefully. They should be light in construction, strong, without arms, and designed to fit the human body. The best type of chair is the type often described in furniture catalogs as a "Youth Chair" or "Junior Chair." Fourteen-inch chairs go with 24-inch tables, 16-inch chairs go with 26-inch tables, and 18-inch chairs go with 28-inch tables. It is not a good plan to cut down chairs of adult size to conform to these heights because the seats are too large. Chairs should be equipped with rubber tips or steel gliders with rubber cushions to minimize noise. Gliders help to protect the floor covering.

Bulletin boards. The library needs to have at least one large bulletin board about 3 feet by 10 feet in size. Other smaller boards may be fitted into wall spaces which are not suitable for shelving. Bulletin boards should be placed low enough for children to see with ease the materials which are displayed. The best material for bulletin boards is the cork material manufactured especially for this purpose. However, a number of fabricated wall boards, such as "celotex" or "masonite," make very satisfactory bulletin boards and are less expensive than the cork. If one of these is used, a type should be selected which is from one-half inch to three-fourths inch thick. It should have a smooth pinning surface, and the texture should be soft enough to take pins and thumbtacks.

Chalkboards. A chalkboard may be very convenient for the librarian when she is explaining to children alphabetical filing of catalog cards, how indexes are arranged, how to make bibliographies, how to take notes, or some other phase of library usage. She may even need it in her storytelling hour. Sometimes a portable board is satisfactory. Combination chalkboards and bulletin boards are now available which can fit over a section of the shelving. It is not advisable to utilize any wall space for permanent chalkboards in the library since all such space is needed for shelving.

Librarian's desk. In the small school, a regular teacher's desk will suffice for the librarian. By the addition of a small table, it can also serve as the charging desk. For the large school, a regular charging desk can be purchased from a dealer in library furniture. An ingenious librarian may wish to design a combination desk and charging desk and have it built by a local cabinetmaker. In a large school, the librarian will probably place her desk in the workroom, and the only desk in the library will be the charging desk.

*Primary grade children enjoy
their library corner.*

*Children assume responsibility
for circulating books.*

Card catalog case. The card catalog case should be purchased from a reliable dealer in library equipment. The sectional type of case is most practical since it can be increased as needed. All drawers in the catalog case should be equipped with rods to hold the cards in place. The size of the card catalog case needed depends entirely upon the size of the book collection. A fair estimate of the size of the case needed may be made by assuming that each book will average from four to five cards in the catalog and that each drawer will accommodate approximately eight hundred cards with sufficient space left for convenience in handling. There is always the danger of purchasing a card catalog case which is too small. It is well to buy the case in separate units keeping in mind the anticipated book collection. It is better to have a number of drawers only partially filled with cards than to have a few drawers packed to capacity.

Book troughs. Two types of portable book troughs are useful. A lightweight trough with handles, made of plywood, is useful for carrying books to and from the classroom. A heavier, more durable type is useful for displaying books in the library and in classrooms. Both types of troughs can be made successfully in the school shops.

A book trough on wheels, available from a dealer in library furniture, may be useful in large schools or in any school where many books need to be transported long distances to classrooms.

Vertical file. Even the smallest library has need for a vertical file to house its collection of pictures and pamphlets. This file should always be legal size since many fugitive materials do not fit conveniently into a letter-size file. This file may be either of steel or wood and should always be purchased from a reliable dealer. Drawers of this size made in local shops frequently do not operate satisfactorily when filled with materials.

Typewriter. Every school library needs a good standard typewriter for typing cards, book lists, bulletin board materials, and for other necessary clerical work.

Magazine shelving. Excellent magazine shelving can be a built-in feature of the library. There are also useful and attractive magazine racks of various sizes and designs which can be purchased from dealers in library equipment. The type of shelving will depend entirely upon the space available in the room, but it is essential that adequate provision be made for correct housing of the magazines.

Dictionary stand. If there is no space available for a separate dictionary stand designed especially for children, a revolving stand can be placed on one of the tables. For all practical purposes this revolving stand is quite sufficient, since reference work in an elementary school does not require extensive use of an unabridged dictionary. Both types of dictionary stands can be purchased from dealers in library equipment.

Charging tray. A double, wooden tray designed especially to hold bookcards in an upright position is the best type of charging tray. This tray is essential as soon as books are circulated from the library. It holds the cards of all books checked out of the room.

Shelf label holders. Shelf labels are needed as soon as books are classified and placed on the shelves. They aid children greatly in locating books. The best type of shelf label holder is of metal and is nailed to the shelf. These can be purchased from any library supply house. One shelf label holder should be placed in the middle of each shelf, and the label in it should indicate the type of books on the shelf above.

Book support. The best type of book support is of metal with rounding corners. These supports can be purchased in two sizes, one for regular size books and an oversize type for large books such as encyclopedias. They may be purchased in various colors. There should be a book support on each shelf to hold the books in an upright position.

Rubber stamp. A rubber stamp with the name of the school library is a necessity for every library. The words can be so arranged as to form an artistic signature. If the letters are too large, the signature becomes unsightly.

Arrangement of furniture

Arranging the furniture in the library requires skill. Important considerations are light, economy of space, convenience, and ease of supervision. Balance is essential for beauty and atmosphere. Large pieces of furniture should parallel the walls. Tables should be placed with the ends toward the windows to insure the best light. The card catalog case and the vertical file need to be near the librarian's desk for convenience. Stands for potted plants should never be placed where they interfere with the regular traffic. Sufficient space should be provided between tables to allow for normal movement. If the library room has a large bay window or a fire-place, this particular corner lends itself to special treatment and can become the most attractive nook in the entire school. It might be provided with rugs, tables, a reading lamp, footstools, comfortable overstuffed chairs of children's size, and pillows. An air of complete informality and beauty will greatly enhance the joy of reading. Fortunate indeed is the child who might have such a nook to remember as a regular part of his elementary school days.

Sources of library supplies

Special library supplies should be purchased from a library supply firm and not from the ordinary stationery store. These include such items as catalog cards, bookcards, bookpockets, date slips, ink for lettering, or electric stylus, white shellac, wood alcohol, stamp pads, date stamp, charging guide cards, pamphlet binders, pressboard guides for vertical file, etc. If the librarian is charged with mending the books, she will need mending supplies also. All such supplies can be found listed in a library supply catalog. Other supplies, such as paper for mounting pictures, pencils, ink, blotters, rubber bands, paper clips, erasers, crayons, and paints, can be obtained from the regular school supply room.

HOW A CLASSROOM MAY BECOME A LIBRARY

If an elementary school has been built without a library, it becomes necessary to convert some room into a library. A school is fortunate if it has some large room which can be given over to the library. Often, however, the only rooms available are classrooms, and it becomes necessary to rebuild a traditional classroom into a library. An excellent library, which will house a collection of two thousand or more books and will accommodate about forty children at one time, can be developed from an ordinary classroom. This converting of a square, dull, and uninteresting room into a bright, cheerful library is a thrilling experience and one which challenges the imagination and artistry of the person in charge.

The physical setup of the room must be carefully planned. The room should be considered from the point of view of size, accessibility, light, amount of unbroken wall space, convenience, plumbing facilities, and "makeover" possibilities in general.

Long blackboards should be removed or covered with inexpensive wallboard or plywood, and chalk trays should be removed. This space becomes the background for shelving. The shelving should be standard as described on page 46. However, it may be necessary to alter the standard length of shelves slightly in order to have them fit into the particular space available. For example, on a wall space of 14 feet, it is impossible to build five standard 3-foot sections of shelving. It is better to divide the space equally into five sections of shelving, 2 feet 9 inches in length, rather than to build four standard 3-foot sections and one section of short shelves. It is usually possible to find space for special shelving for oversize books and for magazines. At least one section of the wall space should be kept clear for a bulletin board.

Large pieces of furniture, such as the vertical file and the card catalog case, can be placed so that they give the appearance of belonging in the room. There is often space at the end of the rows of windows on one side of the room for such pieces of furniture.

The cloakroom can be converted into a workroom by the addition of a sink, some standard shelving, and other facilities for which there may be space. It may be desirable to wall up one of the doorways of the cloakroom, thus giving space for magazine shelving.

THE LIBRARY CORNER IN THE CLASSROOM

Many classrooms are now being built with facilities for shelving books. Usually bookshelves are built into a corner of the room. This corner can be equipped and arranged so that it is truly a "room library." The corner may be either at the front of the room or at the back. The important thing is to develop the library corner in a place where it will interfere least with the normal use of the room and where children using the library corner will be disturbed least by recitations and other regular class activities. All shelving should be standard, and, if possible, there should be a bulletin board at the side for special book announcements and news. A library table and chairs are desirable in this corner. A round table may fit into the space better than a rectangular table, and it will lend an informal atmosphere. If no shelves are provided, a table and chairs can be placed in a corner of the room and the books placed in portable book troughs on the table.

DECORATIVE FEATURES OF THE LIBRARY

The physical setup of the library has much to do with the general attractiveness of the room. It is difficult to achieve much beauty in a room in which the shelves sag or the furniture and equipment have been built with little thought to either utility or beauty of design. Even the most artistically planned and beautifully furnished library can be made unattractive by the kind of decorations used in the room.

Simplicity in decorations

Furnishings, equipment, and decorations do not need to be expensive. The most important requirements are that the room be furnished comfortably and adequately for the purpose to which it is dedicated and that it be pleasing in appearance. Simplicity should be the keynote in all decoration, and simple rules of balance, line, rhythm, and all-around good taste must be kept in mind. It is not possible to add beauty to the room with pictures hung above the top shelves, bouquets of flowers in every available space, figurines and statuettes tucked in nooks and corners, bulletin boards crowded with displays, and window sills cluttered with book troughs and plants. Such decorations result in an atmosphere of confusion and are distracting even though they may represent an honest attempt to add attractiveness and "library atmosphere."

Equally futile are attempts to beautify the library by hanging a few permanent art masterpieces purchased hastily from some bargain house and by supplementing this decoration with potted plants and "long lasting" bulletin board displays. One needs only to study the window displays of fine shops to observe the simplicity and beauty of their decoration. Few items are displayed at one time, so few, in fact, that the observer remembers just what is the theme of the decoration. Gone are the days when a sample of every article for sale in the store has a permanent place in the main window. Just as the decorator studies his public, so the librarian must study hers—a public quite as critical. Just as the decorator must decide on a theme, on color, on timeliness, on how much space he can afford to give to certain displays, so must the librarian give time and thought to these very same decisions. If the librarian has little artistic sense, she can at least apply the principle of simplicity in decoration.

Permanent decorations

Framed pictures, statuary, curtains or drapes, potted plants, pottery, and other art objects are the most common types of permanent decorations one observes in school libraries. None of these is essential as a means of decoration. Properly used, they may add beauty to a room, but as often as not they add a discordant note to the room due to inappropriateness of selection and poor placing of the objects.

There are many good reproductions of art masterpieces available at rather modest prices, if one is searching for framed pictures for library decoration. Making a selection is a difficult job, however, since it involves a careful consideration not only of what type of picture will appeal to children but also of what pictures are appropriate as permanent fixtures in an elementary school library. It involves a consideration of where the picture can be hung in the room so that it has sufficient space and correct light. Pictures must be hung low enough for the children to see. They must have space so that their beauty is not dimmed by some other decoration placed close by. The light must be right or it will reflect on the glass and ruin the whole effect.

Statuary has little place in the decorative scheme of the library. The remarks about the selection of framed pictures hold true for statuary, except that statuary cannot be purchased inexpensively. There is a definite place, however, for inexpensive figurines. These are attractive to display with an appropriate book and add real interest in the book. The alert and artistic librarian is a steady customer of the dime store, for there she will find, from time to time, interesting and attractive figurines useful in decoration and appealing to the children.

Curtains and drapes for the most part add little beauty to the room and tend to shut out light. If used at all, they should be simple in design. Rods which swing back against the wall are particularly good for hanging curtains and drapes since they allow for the maximum of light and air.

Whether there is a place for potted plants in the library depends entirely upon the type of room and the exposure of the windows. If plants are used, they should be used sparingly and must be tended carefully so that they are really beautiful. They should be placed so that they in no way interfere with the free and natural movement of the children about the room. In localities where cut flowers are not plentiful, potted plants may provide the only plant life in the room. They can be beautiful and give enjoyment if they are carefully selected and cared for, well placed, and are few in number.

There is always a place for cut flowers in the library. Even the beauty of flowers can be marred by lack of artistry in arranging and placing them, and the most ordinary weeds may be made to look beautiful if they are attractively arranged. There are many books available on flower arrangement which contain sketches and photographs of actual arrangements. The librarian will do well to study some of these books in order to get new ideas on how to make even the most beautiful flowers more beautiful. As in most decoration, the keynote is simplicity. In some schools, children are given instruction on the care and arrangement of cut flowers in art or science classes. These children will prove willing and clever helpers. No matter how beautiful an arrangement of flowers, it must be discarded as soon as it begins to fade. Better no flowers at all than a half dead reminder of something once beautiful.

Exhibits and bulletin board displays, which are so important a part of the decorative features of the library, are discussed fully in the next chapter.

General appearance

Good housekeeping has much to do with the general appearance of any room. In the library this entails attention to special details which do not appear in the ordinary classroom. Books must be kept upright on the shelves and standing flush with the edge of the shelves. Chairs and tables need to be kept in order. Shelves, tables, chairs, and books must be kept dusted. Papers, posters, and flat materials should never be stored on open shelves because of the disorder they produce. Clean floors and windows are expected at all times.

chapter **6**

Library publicity

and promotion

The success of publicizing the library and its resources depends upon the ingenuity and enthusiasm of the librarian, for it is her responsibility to make both children and teachers aware of what the library has to offer. With the principal, she shares the responsibility of informing parents about the importance of the library in the life of their children. She has innumerable opportunities during the school year to come before parents' groups with her "wares." Book Week presents an opportune time for her to sponsor a special program for the Parent-Teacher Association, the Mothers' Club, or the Room Mothers. The program may be a play which she and the children have worked on cooperatively, a play designed to show the parents how children learn to use the card catalog, the reference books, or the resources of the audio-visual section. The program may consist of groups of children dramatizing scenes or interpreting characters from their favorite books. It may consist of book reviews by the children. It may take the form of an exhibit with children in charge, telling about the various types of books and audio-visual materials which the library offers. The librarian, with the help of the children, may prepare lists of books suggested for Christmas gifts and present these lists to parents before the Christmas season. Parents may be invited to hold one of their meetings each year in the library, at which time children explain about the library and the activities centered around it.

Possibilities for this type of publicity are many. A little planning on the part of the principal and the librarian will bring excellent results. Enthusiasm is contagious, and interested parents will do much to augment the library program of any school.

Publicizing the library to teachers has been discussed in Chapter 3. Library-minded teachers and truly interested principals make excellent publicity agents for the library. They often see opportunities to advertise books and expand the services of the library which the librarian may miss entirely. And the best promotors of the library program are the enthusiastic users of the library—the children themselves!

EXHIBITS

Exhibits have a definite place in the modern elementary school and they offer a fine medium for library publicity. The scope of materials exhibited may be as broad or as narrow as the vision the teachers have of the value of visual materials in teaching children. There will be exhibits in the classrooms. There will be exhibits in the hallways or in the auditorium, and there will be exhibits in the library. These exhibits may grow out of classroom work or activities and represent the work of children. They may be materials loaned by teachers or friends of the school or borrowed from a central visual education department and may or may not supplement the work which is being carried on in the various classrooms. No matter what the exhibit is or where it is displayed, it offers a challenge to the librarian to set up in the library a display of books which pertain to the exhibit. Some "catchy" phrase or notice about the books will add interest both to the exhibit and to the books.

Even in the smallest library, arrangements can be made for special exhibits of books. The top shelf of the low shelving provides space. There is often a shelf under the bulletin board. An additional table may be moved into the room, or even empty shelves may be utilized. Such book exhibits may center around almost any subject or theme. They may develop as the result of some classroom project or a special holiday. (See "Suggested subjects for bulletin board displays," p.62.) Any exhibit of books can be enlivened by the addition of suitable realia. Realia of all types may be used: dolls, toys, models, handcrafts of all types, whatever the librarian or children might think of as being descriptive of the books exhibited. The help of teachers and children in providing realia for display will add to school interest in the exhibits.

Hobby exhibits are most appropriate for library display since there are books for every hobby. Children are very proud to provide the library with an exhibit of their "priceless possessions," and very often it is through a hobby exhibit that the librarian comes to understand a particular child for the first time. Displaying a few books with a hobby exhibit is a good way to gain the interest of some children in books and reading. Children often make collections of useless materials and objects, and therefore the librarian will have to be careful in her selections of children's hobbies for exhibition in the library. The purpose of all library exhibits is to further reading and library activities. Many elementary schools hold a hobby day once a year in which all children in the school are invited to participate. This provides the incentive for bulletin board displays and book exhibits in the library.

The following are important points to be observed in setting up and maintaining exhibits in the library:

Attempt only one thing at a time.

Begin work on the exhibit far enough in advance to have everything organized before beginning to set up the exhibit.

Show only what can be handled well in the space available.

Place the exhibit so that it will not interfere with free movement about the room.

Arrange the exhibit in an artistic manner so that it in no way gives the room a cluttered appearance.

Be sure there are enough labels to explain the exhibit.

Remove the exhibit when interest in it begins to decrease.

A glass exhibit case is not necessary for an elementary school library, but if it has been provided as part of the library equipment it is essential that it house only displays which are of real interest to children. Child interest will be maintained in the case more successfully if it is utilized for very special types of exhibits only and if it is removed from the room when it is not in use.

BULLETIN BOARD DISPLAYS

The bulletin board, artistically presented and arranged, can become the most important publicity device used by the librarian. The ultimate aim of every display placed on the bulletin board is to further the child's interest in books and reading. The board is a utility board, yet it must present its visual materials artistically. It will sell itself if it is properly located, if the displays have singleness of purpose, and if it arouses child interest. The simple display is invariably the most effective one. It is far better to center the entire display around one theme than to attempt to put over several ideas on the bulletin board at one time. An appropriate heading will invariably add to the attractiveness and success of the display (*see* list of suggestions, p.62, and illustrations, p.63).

If there is more than one bulletin board, it is a good idea to set aside one for birthdays of children's authors and illustrators or for special news events. No matter how fine the displays on the bulletin boards, interest will be maintained only if there is frequent change of material.

Pupil participation in planning and arranging the bulletin board displays should be encouraged. This may be accomplished through committees of children from the various classrooms or through committees selected by the librarian. Some child should be appointed chairman of each committee, but the librarian should supervise all plans for displays. The librarian's active participation as a member of the committee and her subtle guidance of the work will result in a very happy relationship with the children. Such a plan always creates and extends interest in the library. The librarian may want to consult with the art teachers for suggestions, and the chairman of the committee may wish to invite the art teachers to sit with the committee when they make plans for the displays or arrange the display on the board. A consideration for color, balance, line, and rhythm is essential to the artistic presentation of any display on the bulletin board.

Materials related to holidays and anniversaries form so important a phase of exhibits and bulletin board displays that librarians find constant need for reference materials on these subjects.

Anniversaries and Holidays,[1] by Mary Emogene Hazeltine, is the most comprehensive discussion of the subject which is suitable for use in elementary schools. It contains a calendar of days which lists

---

[1] Mary Emogene Hazeltine, *Anniversaries and Holidays: A Calendar of Days and How to Observe Them* (2d ed.; Chicago: American Library Association, 1944).

birthdays of notable people, holidays, and special occasions. It also contains much interesting material on the origin and history of holidays and holiday customs.

The Children's Almanac of Books and Holidays,[2] compiled by Helen Dean Fish, is an unusual and useful guide. The material is presented in the form of an old almanac and lists events and birthdays important in the history of children's literature.

Compton's Pictured Encyclopedia[3] contains a good article entitled "Festivals and Holidays" which lists, according to months, holidays and festivals observed in the United States and refers to additional information in other articles on some of the specific holidays. The article also contains information about the most important foreign holidays and celebrations.

The World Book Encyclopedia[4] lists a calendar of birthdays and events under the name of each month. These articles about each month discuss special days which occur during the month and refer to other articles in the encyclopedia which give additional information.

The Children's Book Council, 50 West 53d St., New York, N. Y., issues a free quarterly *Calendar* which not only lists special weeks and events but also gives interesting news about books, their authors, illustrators, and publishers. A most useful pamphlet entitled *Book Displays—January to December,* available from the North Carolina Department of Public Instruction, Raleigh, N. C., for 25 cents a copy, gives useful information on how to make and set up displays and exhibits.

The following suggestions may be found helpful in the preparation of bulletin board displays.

Arrangement

There should be a center of interest for each bulletin board display.

Margins of the bulletin board should be balanced.

The material should be balanced. The edges next to the outside margins should usually be straight and the lowest margin should invariably be the widest.

---

[2] Helen Dean Fish, comp., *The Children's Almanac of Books and Holidays* (New York: Frederick A. Stokes, 1934). Also in Stanley J. Kunitz, ed., *The Junior Book of Authors* (New York: H. W. Wilson, 1934).
[3] *Compton's Pictured Encyclopedia* (Chicago: F. E. Compton, 1954).
[4] *The World Book Encyclopedia* (Chicago: Field Enterprises, 1954).

An appropriate heading adds to the meaning and attractiveness. When finished, the display, as a whole, should constitute a picture pleasing to the eye.

Color

Color adds much to the attractiveness of bulletin boards when wisely used. It may be gained in mounts for headings and pictures and by the use of colored letters.

Lettering

All lettering should be large and legible.

Handmade letters are most effective. Cutout letters can be made from squares of paper by children in art classes. Several sets of letters of the same style of lettering and color are recommended. They can be used over and over again. Explicit yet simple directions for cutout letters are given in *Free-Hand Paper Cutting*, by Cornelia Carter.[5]

Pins are recommended for holding letters on the board. They are less conspicuous than thumbtacks.

Mounting

The beauty of most pictures is increased when mounted on a harmonious background of colored paper or papers.

Pasting permanent mountings of paper on pictures and book jackets is wasteful of paper and renders the material useless for certain color schemes. For this reason pins are recommended for all mountings. The material to be mounted may be placed on top of the colored paper and held in place by pins in each corner. This method permits the re-use of both the display material and the colored paper. When pictures are mounted, the lower margin should always be the widest.

Materials for display

Colored pictures, book jackets, posters, and maps are most effective, especially when tastefully mounted. In using advertisements, remove all printing if possible.

Enlargements of pictures, illustrations from books, or entire book jackets supply a stimulating center for a display. (*See* "Book

[5] Cornelia Carter, *Free-Hand Paper Cutting* (Bloomington, Ill.: McKnight and McKnight, 1944).

jackets," p.104.) Enlargements can be made easily with an opaque projector. These enlargements can be made on white paper and later colored, or can be drawn directly on colored paper. Children can do this work successfully.

Posters and drawings made by children are also suitable materials for display. Art classes can cooperate by making book posters and book illustrations.

With clippings, large, clear type is essential. A few well-selected clippings on one topic are more likely to be read than many on a variety of subjects.

Typewritten materials, such as short poems, quotations, puzzles, and parts of stories, may be used for display. Use a primer typewriter or one with pica type.

Photographs are also appropriate for bulletin board displays. Children who take kodak pictures might enjoy displaying them.

Suggested subjects for bulletin board displays

Any subject in which the children are interested will afford suitable material for bulletin board displays. The following subjects are typical:

Animals	Holidays and special seasons
Biography	Indians
Birds	Magazines
Birthdays of the month	Material correlating with class-
Book characters	room work
Book week	New books
Book illustrators and illustrations	News of the city library
Explorations	Pets
Hobbies	Sports

Examples of effective bulletin board displays

The following are descriptions of actual displays which have been used in an elementary school library.

New Year. Six sheets of a large calendar, with two months on each sheet, were placed on the board in a large oval pattern. Seven book jackets were tucked in between the calendar sheets in an informal arrangement. A large caption at the top read, "Good the Calendar Round."

A large circle of braided, colored cord was placed in the center of the board in the form of a key ring from which hung four large

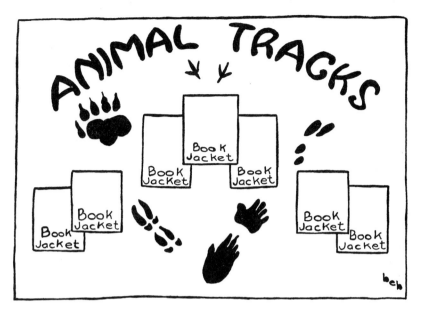

Sample bulletin board displays

keys cut from colored construction paper. Each key was labeled
with the name of one of the four seasons. Book jackets were
arranged in groups of three around the key ring. The caption
was "Good Reading Any Season."

February. Timely for Valentine's Day was a clock made of twelve red hearts. The title of a book and call number were written in white chalk on each heart. The hands of the clock were made of white cord ending with a tiny heart. The hands pointed to two books and the caption was "Time to Read."

Combining Valentine's Day with February birthdays of famous people was a huge red heart, edged with halves of paper doilies. Three large rents in the heart showed pictures of Washington, Lincoln, and Edison. The caption was "February's Famous." Suitable books were displayed below the bulletin board.

Easter. A large bunny was cut from construction paper. He wore yellow trousers, a green jacket, and a necktie of purple satin ribbon. He pulled a two-wheeled cart of light green construction paper filled with book jackets. The caption was "Mr. Bunny Brings Books."

Halloween. Ten-inch black letters spelled "Look." The "o's" had white centers cut to represent eyeballs, giving the word a spooky expression. A pyramid of book jackets topped by a black cat looking at the two eyes in the word "Look" completed the display. The book jackets were of cat stories.

Thanksgiving. A large turkey was cut from construction paper. His fan-like tail and drooping wing were fashioned of book jackets. Autumn leaves made of colored construction paper were added to complete the picture. The caption read "A Thanksgiving Menu."

Christmas. Large Christmas tree ornaments were cut from gold, silver, and shiny colored paper. The ornaments were pinned to the bulletin board but were attached to a thick cord of green and silver tinsel. A Christmas book jacket was placed in the center of each ornament.

The imaginative librarian, with suggestions from a committee of children, can arrange many interesting displays around such headings as: We Are Waiting for You; Tops in Tales; Books March On; Laugh, Clown, Laugh; Bushels of Good Reading; Our Yesteryears; Animal Tracks; Here, There, and Everywhere; Books to Tackle; Walking with the Great; You Can't Beat These; This Land I Love.

*Children's art work is used
for display.*

Bulletin board displays
give opportunity
for student participation.

chapter 7

Selecting books

and magazines

Selecting books for the school library is one of the most important phases of elementary school library work. It is a task which no one person can accomplish alone, since it affects the entire personnel of the school. Selecting books wisely should invariably involve the cooperation of principal, teachers, supervisors, public librarian, school librarian, and children. The librarian must utilize the knowledge of various members of the faculty in their special fields. If there is a public library, she may get much valuable information from the librarian of the children's department. She will need to review and read children's books continuously in order to be familiar with books which are constantly being published. In addition to the information available from professional sources, valuable information can be obtained from the children on the kinds of books they like and want as a permanent part of their library.

Books in the school library fall into two general classes in terms of the purpose for which the children will use the books. One class comprises recreational reading books, the other reference or supplementary books needed for classroom work. Both types of books must be carefully selected from the standpoint of pupil interest. Many books fall distinctly into one or the other of these classes, but many others are used in both types of reading. Children will develop a real companionship with books only when they find in their experience that books please and delight them.

The school librarian is ordinarily regarded as the book authority of the school because of her special training in the field. However, it is quite impossible to obtain a complete understanding of children's books from a course or two in "Children's Literature." The field of children's books is a large and growing field in the publishing world. It is one which requires constant study by the school librarian in order that she may select wisely from the vast numbers of new books which appear each year. Even in the group of so-called "classics," the librarian faces a constant problem of discrimination in book selection. Many books which were favorites of the present adult generation when they were children may have no appeal to children today. Too often the one who selects books for children, be it parent, teacher, or librarian, selects those books which he thinks the children *should* like, those which he himself liked as a child, or those he likes now as an adult. Above all, one who selects books for children must keep in mind the children themselves, their interests and their needs.

Children have a definite feeling for books, and they have standards for judging their books although they may not be able to define their standards clearly. They like books which stir the imagination, books with plenty of humor, books which express the kinds of experiences they would like to have, books of excitement, and books which express a conviction of real decency, of courage, and of honesty in the characters. They demand authenticity and up-to-dateness in books which deal with science, aviation, and industrial developments. We cannot predict which of the modern books for children will live to become classics. We only know that the books which will live to gain that label of recognition will be the books which the children themselves choose to keep alive.

While some of the factors involved in the selection of a school library book collection may appear rather subjective and abstract, others are quite definite and objective. Let us consider briefly some of these factors:

1. *The size of the book collection is definitely related to the enrollment of the school.* However, there are no set standards as to what constitutes the correct number of books per pupil in an elementary school library. An excellent library can be established on the basis of from three to five volumes per pupil enrolled, provided the books are selected carefully. Of course, the larger the book col-

lection the better. A large, well-selected book collection makes possible such services as home circulation, larger circulation to classrooms, and an appeal to a wider field of children's interests. In building the book collection it is important to bear in mind the ultimate size of the collection which is being planned. A different problem of selection is involved in planning a library of 2000 volumes and one of 10,000 volumes.

2. *There is a definite relationship between the book budget and the number of volumes which can be purchased and maintained.* A good working estimate for the cost of a library collection can be arrived at by figuring the cost of books at about two dollars per volume. While many of the books will cost less than this, other books such as encyclopedias, unabridged dictionaries, and beautifully illustrated editions of certain titles will make up the difference. The entire book budget can never be spent for new titles. From 20 to 25 per cent of the annual expenditure in the average library will be required for replacement of worn out titles. The American Library Association recommends an annual minimum maintenance budget of one dollar and fifty cents per pupil enrolled. It also recommends a minimum active collection of five books per pupil.[1]

3. *The book collection should bear direct relationship to the course of study and to the teaching techniques of the school.* It is apparent that reference or supplementary books used in connection with classroom work should bear direct relationship to the course of study. If the sixth-grade social studies course centers about the United States, children and teachers will need many books about the United States. If teachers and children engage in classroom work involving many activities, the library must be in a position to furnish the necessary books and information. It is a waste of money to build up any phase of the book collection which is not functioning in the life of the school.

4. *The book collection should be balanced as to subject fields and reading levels. It should contain books of real literary worth for recreational reading as well as reference and supplementary books for classroom work.* A library which consists in the main of shelves filled with readers, geographies, histories, language books, and health books can never be considered a true library. While the

---

[1] American Library Association, *School Libraries for Today and Tomorrow: Functions and Standards* (Chicago: The Association, 1945).

modern elementary school library should have an extensive collection of supplementary books for classroom circulation, this should never be maintained at the expense of the general library collection for recreational reading. Children will never develop a feeling for books, a lasting interest in reading for pleasure, and the habit of using library materials as sources of information if they have at their disposal only supplementary texts and reference books. Constant thought and attention must therefore be given to the book collection in order to maintain a wholesome balance between supplementary books and books for recreational reading.

Equally important in the development of the library book collection is the maintenance of balance in various subject fields and fields of children's interests. Unless this matter is carefully controlled it is easy for one subject field or some limited field of interest to absorb a major portion of the book budget.

Books in the various fields must represent a wide variety of reading levels. A boy in the seventh grade with a fourth-grade reading ability may be interested in aviation. His need is for books on aviation on his particular reading level. A girl in the fifth grade, reading at the eighth-grade level, who is interested in historical fiction, can satisfy her interest only with books written in a more mature manner than books written for the average fifth-grade child. If children are to seek answers to their classroom problems through the medium of the printed page, various levels of reading also must be represented in books for reference or supplementary reading. Give the book collection scope as to subject fields and breadth as to reading levels if you would seek to serve all the children.

5. *The book collection should be planned to serve the individual needs and interests of the children.* It is impossible to stress too strongly the importance of keeping in mind individual children, their interests and their needs, when selecting books for the school library. There must be books to extend and enrich the experiences of every child who comes to read. To care for such varied interests and abilities, the collection must contain books in every field of knowledge. Fortunate are the children of today, for they are the first generation of children who have had books written especially for them in practically every known field of knowledge. Outstanding authors are writing fine story books of the contemporary scene, authoritative books in the fields of science, radio, aviation, biography, and history.

Use of book selection aids

A very important matter in the development of a book collection is the intelligent and effective use of available book selection aids. The field of children's books is so large that it is impossible for even the best-trained and enthusiastic school librarian to know firsthand all of the books. The problem is further complicated by the large number of new books which are published each year. Those who select books must, therefore, rely on book lists and book reviews and must be familiar with the authoritative book selection aids. There are a large number of book lists available and the beginning librarian may be at a loss to know which of these will serve as the most reliable guides. She also must discriminate between descriptive lists and those which evaluate. Publishers' catalogs are always descriptive and are issued as a regular part of the advertising program of the company.

A descriptive list of reliable book and nonbook selection aids will be found in: Joint Committee of the National Education Association and the American Library Association, comps., *Aids in Selection of Materials: Books, Films, Records, for Children and Young People* (Chicago: American Library Association, 1952), 10c.

BOOK LISTS

The basic book collection

The following recognized book lists will be found invaluable to anyone who is selecting books for the basic book collection:

A Basic Book Collection for Elementary Grades, compiled by a Joint Committee of the American Library Association, National Education Association, National Council of Teachers of English, and Association for Childhood Education. Miriam Snow, chairman. Chicago: American Library Association, 1951. $2.

> One thousand selected books are arranged under subjects, and described briefly, with grade levels for each. Includes picture books and easy books. Full buying information is given. Indexed by author, title, and subject.

A Basic Book Collection for Junior High Schools, compiled by Elsa R. Berner and Mabel S. Sacra. Chicago: American Library Association, 1950. $1.75.

> A selection of books suggested for first purchase for a small junior high school. Arranged by subject. Annotated and indexed. Buying information and classification are given.

A Bibliography of Books for Children. 1952 revision. Washington,
D. C.: Association for Childhood Education International, 1953. $1.
> A selected, classified list of books for elementary school children.
> Annotated. Includes prices.

Children's Catalog, compiled by Ruth Giles and Dorothy E. Cook. 8th
ed. New York: H. W. Wilson, 1951. Sold on service basis. Write for
price.
> Contains over 3000 children's books selected and annotated for
> library and school use. Gives subject headings and classification.
> Titles recommended for first purchase are starred. Complete re-
> vision every five years.

Two other publications, although planned especially as indexes
to readers, textbooks, and other selected books, are also very useful
as aids in selecting the basic book collection. For this reason they
are listed in this section dealing with recognized book lists. These
publications are:

Rue, Eloise, comp. *Subject Index to Books for Intermediate Grades.*
2d ed. Chicago: American Library Association, 1950. $6.
> Indexes, under subjects and units, material in over 1800 text and
> trade books recommended for fourth, fifth, and sixth grades. Stars
> 215 books for small library first purchase. Gives grade range for
> each reference. Alphabetical list of books indexed gives full buying
> information.

Rue, Eloise, comp. *Subject Index to Books for Primary Grades.* Chicago: American Library Association, 1943. $2.50. First supplement;
Chicago: American Library Association, 1946. $1.25. (Combined price
of both items, $3.)
> Indexes, under subject, material in readers, picture books, and story
> books recommended for first three grades. 225 of these titles pub-
> lished between 1942 and 1946. Gives grade range for each refer-
> ence. Alphabetical list of books indexed gives full buying informa-
> tion.

Current books

An important phase of book selection in any library is the selection of current titles. New books are constantly appearing and it is
necessary to provide for new interests of children and the changing
school program. Fortunately there are a number of dependable
periodicals which review current books. The following are a few of
the best guides to new books:

The Booklist: A Guide to Current Books. Chicago: American Library Association. Semimonthly. $6 a year.

> Current books for children, young people, and adults which are recommended for school libraries are described critically. Gives classification, subject headings, and full buying information. Age range is given for children's and young people's books. Includes lists of free and inexpensive material.

Elementary English. Chicago: National Council of Teachers of English. Monthly from October to May. $3.50 a year.

> Official organ of the National Council of Teachers of English. Frequently prints book lists on special subjects, and often contains articles on children's books and authors.

Horn Book Magazine. Boston: Horn Book, Inc. Bimonthly. $3.50 a year.

> Devoted to children's literature exclusively. In addition to reviews of new books, it contains articles about authors, illustrators, and the publishing of children's books.

Library Journal. New York: R. R. Bowker. Issued twice a month. $6 a year.

> Part II of the regular feature, "New Books Appraised," is "Children's Books Appraised by Children's Librarians." It contains signed annotations by children's and school librarians throughout the country.

New York Herald Tribune Book Review. New York: New York Herald Tribune. Weekly. $2 a year.

> "Books for Young People," conducted by Louise Seaman Bechtel, is featured in the Sunday book supplement of the *New York Herald Tribune.*

New York Times Book Review. New York: New York Times. Weekly. $3 a year.

> A section of children's and young people's books edited by Ellen Lewis Buell is a regular feature in the book review section of the Sunday *New York Times.*

Reference books

There are a few standard reference books which will be needed in any modern elementary school which seeks to give teachers and children unlimited service. Reliable information is available about subscription books of all kinds in a bulletin published by the American Library Association. The bulletin is called *Subscription Books Bulletin* and evaluates such books as encyclopedias, sets of books for children, dictionaries, and other books which are ordinarily sold on a subscription basis.

Subscription Books Bulletin. Chicago: American Library Association. Quarterly. $2.50 a year.

> Each set of books is reviewed and is "Recommended," "Recommended with certain qualifications," or "Not recommended." This is the best aid in checking subscription sets, since it contains accurate, unbiased, and outspoken reviews by experts who have given the sets careful examination.

Standard reference books for the elementary school library

The following reference books are indispensable in an elementary school library. The number required will depend upon the size of the school, the course of study, and the program of teaching in the particular school. Reviews and evaluations of these books will be found in book lists already noted in this chapter.

ENCYCLOPEDIAS

Britannica Junior: The Boys' and Girls' Encyclopaedia. Chicago: Encyclopaedia Britannica, 1954. 15 volumes. Library binding, $87.90; special price to schools. (1952 ed. is evaluated in *Subscription Books Bulletin* for January 1953.)

Compton's Pictured Encyclopedia. Chicago: F. E. Compton, 1954. 15 volumes. Dura-cloth binding, $109.50. (1952 ed. is evaluated in *Subscription Books Bulletin* for January 1953.)

World Book Encyclopedia. Chicago: Field Enterprises, 1954. 19 volumes. Roxite binding, $109. (1952 ed. is evaluated in *Subscription Books Bulletin* for January 1953.)

UNABRIDGED DICTIONARIES

Funk & Wagnalls New Standard Dictionary of the English Language. New York: Funk & Wagnalls, 1942. $30. (Reviewed in *Subscription Books Bulletin* for July 1948.)

Webster's New International Dictionary of the English Language. 2d ed. Springfield, Mass.: G. & C. Merriam, 1934. $35. (Reviewed in *Subscription Books Bulletin* for July 1948.)

ABRIDGED DICTIONARIES

The following dictionaries are planned especially for the use of elementary school children:

Thorndike, E. L. *Thorndike-Barnhart Beginning Dictionary.* Chicago: Scott, Foresman, 1952. $2.88. Planned especially for teaching the use of the dictionary. Contains lessons.

Thorndike, E. L. *Thorndike-Barnhart Junior Dictionary.* Chicago: Scott, Foresman, 1952. $2.80.

Walpole, Ellen W. *Golden Dictionary.* New York: Simon & Schuster, 1944. $2.75. Especially useful in teaching English to non-English speaking children and in speech correction classes.

Webster's Elementary Dictionary: A Dictionary for Boys and Girls. New York: American Book, 1935. $2.88.

The Winston Dictionary for Schools. Philadelphia: John C. Winston, 1950. $2.80.

YEARBOOKS

World Almanac and Book of Facts. Latest annual. New York: World-Telegram. $1.85. (Reviewed in *Subscription Books Bulletin* for April 1948.)

Britannica Book of the Year. Chicago: Encyclopaedia Britannica. $4.95, special price for purchasers of *Britannica Junior* for a period of five years. (Reviewed in *Subscription Books Bulletin* for January 1950.)

World Book Encyclopedia Annual. A review of events of the year. Chicago: Field Enterprises. Issued each year. $1.25. (Reviewed in *Subscription Books Bulletin* for January 1950.)

ATLASES

Goode, John Paul. *Goode's World Atlas.* Edited by Edward B. Espenshade, Jr. Chicago: Rand McNally, 1953. $7.25.

Rand McNally Cosmopolitan World Atlas. Chicago: Rand McNally, 1949. $12.50.

AUTHORS AND ILLUSTRATORS

Kunitz, S. J., and Haycraft, Howard. *The Junior Book of Authors.* 2d ed., rev. New York: H. W. Wilson, 1951. $3.50.

Mahony, Bertha E., comp. *Illustrators of Children's Books, 1944-1945.* Boston: Horn Book, 1947. $20.

Young Wings. *Writing Books for Boys and Girls.* Edited by Helen Ferris. Garden City, N. Y.: Junior Literary Guild, Doubleday, 1952. $2.98.

Inexpensive books

Inexpensive books, selling for twenty-five cents to a dollar and fifty cents are appearing in great numbers on a variety of subjects.

These books offer fine opportunities for schools with limited budgets to build up a collection of books with a wide spread of titles for a small expenditure of money. They offer also a fine addition to the large library. Since these books are so inexpensive, soiled copies can be replaced freely at the end of each year. Many of these books are sold in the dime stores side by side with books of trash, and the librarian must apply to these books the same standards of selection as to content and format that she applies in judging the more expensive books. Two excellent lists are available which will be useful in the selection of these inexpensive books:

Adamson, Catherine E., ed. *Inexpensive Books for Boys and Girls.* 3d ed. Chicago: American Library Association, 1952. 65c.
> A buying guide of in-print American and English editions of more than 700 titles suitable for public and elementary school library use. All are priced at $1.50 or less, with the emphasis throughout on editions of lasting value. Gives full information for each entry.

Association for Childhood Education International. *Children's Books for Eighty-five Cents or Less.* Prepared by Elizabeth H. Gross. Washington, D. C.: The Association, 1953. 50c.
> 1953 revision of a classified list of inexpensive, approved books for children. Gives full information for each entry. Indexed.

Reprints and school editions

The Cadmus Books published by E. M. Hale and Company represent one of the best groups of reprints available. They are sold only to schools and school libraries. The list includes a wide variety of titles, ranging in scope from the primary grades through the junior high school grades. Most of the titles on the list appear on recognized standard lists of books for children. The books are printed from the original plates of the original publisher's editions on strong paper with unusual binding reinforcements. The price varies with individual titles, but all are inexpensive.

With the growth of elementary school libraries, the demand for trade books in strong bindings has increased tremendously. As a result of this demand many publishers are now publishing school or educational editions of some of their trade books for children. In most cases these editions are printed on strong paper, the same illustrations are used that appear in the trade editions, the binding is specially reinforced, and the books sell for a much lower price than the original trade editions. They are much more practical for school library use than the trade editions and are highly recommended for purchase.

Magazines and newspapers

There is considerable difference of opinion regarding the place of magazines and newspapers in the elementary school library. Some librarians contend that few children actually read periodicals, that they merely turn the pages idly looking at the advertisements and pictures, and are thus forming wrong habits of reading. Others think that through periodicals the uninterested child or the slow reader may be led into the joys of reading other things. Each school will need to determine its own policy with regard to the expenditure of funds for periodicals.

There are a number of good magazines and newspapers published especially for children. Real help in the selection of them can be found in the section devoted to magazines for the elementary school in *Magazines for School Libraries* by Laura Katherine Martin.[2] The titles listed below are those which have been found useful in many elementary schools. A few titles published primarily for adults have been included because of their valuable pictures or their interest to children in seventh and eighth grades. These titles are starred. Many of these magazines are indexed in *The Subject Index to Children's Magazines,* 301 Palomino Lane, Madison, Wis., which is published monthly except July, with cumulations in February and August. The price is $5 a year; sample copies will be sent upon request. This useful reference tool is reviewed in *Subscription Books Bulletin* for July 1951.

American Boy–Open Road. Holyoke Publishing Co., 420 Lexington Avenue, New York. Monthly. $3.

American Girl. Girl Scouts of the U.S.A., 155 E. 44th Street, New York. Monthly. $2.50 a year.

American Junior Red Cross News. American National Red Cross, Washington, D. C. Monthly. 50c a year.

Boys' Life. Boy Scouts of America, 2 Park Avenue, New York. Monthly. $3 a year.

Child Life. 136 Federal Street, Boston, Mass. Monthly. $3.

Children's Digest. Parents' Institute Inc., 52 Vanderbilt Avenue, New York. Monthly. $3.

---

[2] Laura Katherine Martin, *Magazines for School Libraries* (rev. ed.; New York: H. W. Wilson, 1950).

Horn Book. 250 Boylston Street, Boston, Mass. 6 times a year. $3.50.

Junior Natural History. American Museum of Natural History, Central Park West at 79th Street, New York. Monthly. $1.50.

Junior Scholastic. Scholastic Magazines, 351 Fourth Avenue, New York. Weekly during school year, September through May. 90c a year.

My Weekly Reader. Numbers 1, 2, 3, 4, 5, 6. (Numbers refer to grade levels.) American Education Publications, 400 Front Street, Columbus, Ohio. Weekly. 50c each number, a year.

National Geographic Magazine. National Geographic Society, 1146 16th Street, N. W., Washington, D. C. Monthly. $6.

Nature Magazine. American Nature Association, 1214 16th Street, N. W., Washington, D. C. Monthly. $4.

Newstime. Scholastic Magazines, 351 Fourth Avenue, New York. Weekly during school year, September through May. 80c a year.

Popular Mechanics. Popular Mechanics Co., 200 E. Ontario Street, Chicago. Monthly. $3.50.

Popular Science. Popular Science Publishing Co., 353 Fourth Avenue, New York. Monthly. $3.

Reader's Digest. Reader's Digest Association, Pleasantville, N. Y. Monthly. $3. Price is less for quantity orders for classroom use.

Story Parade. Story Parade, Inc., 630 Fifth Avenue, New York. Monthly. $3.

Publishers' exhibits

Many bookstores and publishers have extended their services by offering to send exhibits of books to schools, as a means of assisting librarians and teachers with their book purchases. Specific titles may be requested by the librarian, or the publishers will make up an exhibit. The exhibit in no way obligates the school to purchase a certain number of books, but books are returned at the close of the exhibit. This type of exhibit is essential in small communities with no bookstores, but it has advantages even in very large city school systems where librarians and teachers are able to visit bookstores. The librarian should be responsible for the exhibit and arrange the display. The auditorium, teacher's room, or principal's office may provide suitable space for it. It may be set up according to subjects or according to grades so that teachers examining the books can readily locate the kinds of books they need. A schedule of teacher visits to the exhibit can be arranged by the principal so that each teacher has time to examine the books in order to make intelligent recommendations for purchase. Children may also participate in selecting books. Book committees may be appointed from each classroom and a schedule made for their visits. Before the visit the teacher should discuss with them the points which they need to observe in examining books. They may discuss with their classmates the kind of books they like and want. After the visit, they can pool their opinions and evaluate their selections. Such cooperative book selection gives both teachers and children a feeling of being an integral part of the school library program. It also gives the librarian real assistance in this phase of her work. The following book recommendation form, mimeographed on 3 x 5 slips, will be found useful to teachers and children for making suggestions to the librarian.

BOOK RECOMMENDATION

Author:

Title:

Publisher:

Recommended by:

    Grade _____

    Name _____

PRINCIPLES OF BOOK SELECTION

Principles of book selection have been taken into consideration by the compilers of the standard book selection aids already discussed. Presumably no title is included in a standard aid which does not meet the highest requisites of fine book selection. However, the school librarian must still exercise careful judgment in choosing from these lists the titles which will best fit the needs of the children and the school program.

There is no substitute for reading or at least examining books before purchasing them. No matter how excellent the annotation, how fine the review, the librarian "feels better" and is able to come to more satisfactory conclusions about ordering books if she has the opportunity to see them. She must learn to read reviews critically, compare the reviews of authorities, and thus add to her own skill in judging the book when she has an opportunity to read or review it.

The following are some questions which must be considered in judging books for children.

Contents of the book

Will the book broaden the child's intellectual and emotional experience?

Will the book appeal to the child's imagination?

If a book of information, is it accurate and up to date? Will it increase the child's knowledge of the subject?

Will it add something new to material already on hand or merely duplicate material?

If a book of fiction, does it give a true picture of life? Do the characters talk and act as real people? Could the story really happen?

Readability of the book

Is the subject matter presented in a suitable manner to the readers for whom it is intended?

Has the author written clearly and simply?

Does the book possess literary style or is it written in a dull and uninteresting manner?

If the book contains factual information, are the facts presented directly or lost in the story or in the conversation?

Physical make-up of the book

Is the book satisfactory as to paper, print, size of type?

Are the illustrations worth while? Do they possess artistic quality?

Is the binding of durable library buckram or a serviceable, washable fabric?

If the book is planned for primary children, is it light in weight and easy to handle?

Does the book look as if it would be interesting to the child audience for which it is planned?

chapter 8

Purchasing books

and magazines

$\mathbf{A}$n important phase of the librarian's work is the actual purchasing of books and periodicals. This phase of the work needs to be carefully organized and systematized, not only for timesaving but also for efficient management of library funds. The details of purchasing will differ in school systems. In school systems with purchasing agents and provisions for central purchasing, the routine will be different from the situation where each individual school orders books separately.

Book fund

It is good policy not to spend the entire book fund on one order. A good plan is to divide the fund so that perhaps three fourths of the money is spent during the summer or early in the fall after a careful study has been made of the requirements of the coming year's program. This expenditure should include replacements as well as new books. The balance of the fund should be held in reserve to meet new needs as they arise. The purchase of a few new books from time to time increases children's interest in the book collection. In school systems which have central purchasing, it is suggested that the large order be placed during the summer so that books will be available for the opening of school.

Organizing book orders

The organization of book orders always presents a definite problem. Unless the matter is efficiently organized there is sure to be confusion in placing orders, in checking the receipt of books, and in keeping records of purchases for future reference. One of the best plans for organizing a book order is to use a card system. This makes it easy to handle the data and assemble the order. Each book to be purchased should be listed on a separate card so that the information about the book can be filed for future reference. School library order cards can be purchased from reliable library supply houses, or the librarian may mimeograph a form card of her own. After the order has been assembled and written, the order cards should be filed to show what books are on order. The following sample card contains all the essential information:

```
Class No. _____    Author _____

No. of copies _____    Title _____

                       Publisher _____

                       Edition _____

                       Date _____

                       Price _____

Ordered from   _____

Date received  _____
```

Sample school library order card

Order form

If the school system has a special form for book purchases, this will be used. If not, the librarian may need to make her own order form. This form should be typewritten on letter-size paper (8½ x 11 inches) and should be tabulated showing number of copies, author, title, edition, publisher, and price. The total amount of the order should be given at the end of the order. The list can be arranged

*Oversize books and magazines require
special shelving.*

Children examine new books and recommend library purchases.

```
                                    School _____

                                    Address _____

                                           _____

                                    Date _____


                        Book Order

Beckley Cardy

      3       Chandler      Cowboy Sam                              1.20      3.60
      2       Comfort       Prairie schooners west                 1.30.     2.60

Doubleday

      1       Roosevelt     Partners, the United Nations and youth            3.00

D. C. Heath

      2       Acacio        Work and play in the Philippines        .48       .96
      2       Desmond       Boys of the Andes                       .48       .96
      1       Williams      Kimbi, Indian of the jungle                       .48

Macmillan

      1       Anderson      A pony for Linda                                  2.00
      1       Bice          Across Canada                                     2.50
      1       Jones         Big Susan                                         3.00
      1       Lathrop       Puppies for keeps                                 2.50
      1       Mason         Timothy has ideas                                 2.00
      1       Sperry        Call it courage                                   2.75
```

Sample order arranged alphabetically by publisher

alphabetically by publisher or by author. Illustrations of two types of order forms are given on this page and page 82.

Placing the order

In some school systems the librarian does not handle book purchases, this detail being handled by the business department. In other systems, however, the librarian must decide where to place the orders. If the librarian is responsible for the purchasing of books, she should be familiar with the various channels through which books may be purchased and should be aware of the advantages and disadvantages of each. The three usual channels she will use are the book jobber or book depository, the local bookstore,

School _____

Address _____

_____

Date _____

Book Order

	Author	Title	Publisher	Unit Price	Total Price
2	Acacio	Work and play in the Philippines	D. C. Heath	.48	.96
1	Anderson	A pony for Linda	Macmillan	2.00	2.00
1	Bice	Across Canada	Macmillan	2.50	2.50
3	Chandler	Cowboy Sam	Beckley Cardy	1.20	3.60
2	Comfort	Prarie schooners west	Beckley Cardy	1.30	2.60
2	Desmond	Boys of the Andes	D. C. Heath	.48	.96
1	Jones	Big Susan	Macmillan	3.00	3.00
1	Lathrop	Puppies for keeps	Macmillan	2.50	2.50
1	Mason	Timothy has ideas	Macmillan	2.00	2.00
1	Roosevelt	Partners, the United Nations and youth	Doubleday	3.00	3.00
1	Sperry	Call it courage	Macmillan	2.75	2.75
1	Williams	Kimbi, Indian of the jungle	D. C. Heath	.48	.48
			Total		26.35

Sample order arranged alphabetically by author

and the book publisher. A reliable book jobber or book depository in a metropolitan area is often preferred since he usually has a large stock of books on hand, consolidates the shipment thus reducing his costs, gives a good discount, and gives prompt and complete service. This type of ordering also cuts down on the amount of clerical work since the entire order goes to one place. A local bookstore or dealer should be patronized if he gives satisfactory service and reasonable discount. His discount may not be as large as that of the book jobber but he will often allow books to go to schools on approval, and a good bookstore in a community deserves the support of the schools. Books may be ordered direct from the publishers. The main advantage of this plan of ordering is that the discounts are usually larger. However, this may be offset by the fact that this type of ordering requires more clerical work since orders for each publisher must be made separately.

Some library books should always be purchased in resewed or reinforced bindings. This applies to books bound in boards, oversize picture books, and certain books which will receive extra hard usage. While this increases the cost of books, the added service will justify the added cost. These books can be purchased through reliable firms which specialize in this type of binding.

The letter to the book jobber, bookstore, or publisher should indicate how the books should be shipped and the number of copies of the invoice required. One copy of the bill should be checked by the librarian and the other copy filed with the principal or business department. Fewer or more copies of the bill may be required according to different school systems. All correspondence with dealers should be attended to promptly and filed for future reference.

Periodicals

Subscriptions for magazines and newspapers should be grouped into one order and sent to a reliable agent or dealer. The order should list the magazines and newspapers alphabetically by title. A dealer will give the best service and offer a good discount. He will also take care of any problems which may come up regarding the subscriptions. It will simplify the renewing of magazine subscriptions if all subscriptions can begin at the same time.

Pamphlets and pictures

Free and inexpensive picture and pamphlet materials can be secured direct from publishers through a request by letter or from a firm which serves as a central distributor. A reliable distributor for pamphlets, booklets, and bulletins is Bacon Pamphlet Service, Northport, Long Island, N. Y. Ordering such materials from one source is a great saving of time and energy and eliminates much clerical detail. If such materials are ordered direct from publishers, it is important that the librarian use official school stationery and sign with her official title. This gives authority to the request. Government publications are secured direct from the Superintendent of Documents, Washington, D. C., and requests must be accompanied by the money to cover payment. Sheets of five-cent coupons which are sold by the Superintendent of Documents are useful in paying for individual orders for publications. These sheets can be ordered and paid for by money order.

chapter 9

Organization of the
book collection

A well-organized library is the first step toward providing effective library service in a school. If the books in the collection have been selected wisely, each book is selected to meet certain specific needs and no book should become misplaced or lost because of poor organization of the collection. The term *well-organized,* used in connection with a library, implies that the book collection is cataloged and classified according to accepted library standards.

Cataloging and classification are highly specialized activities which require definite training on the part of the person who performs them. Unless the person in charge of the elementary school library has had training in this field, she should not be expected to carry out this particular phase of library organization. When such work is carried on by an inexperienced person, it is not only very expensive in time consumed but also likely to be inadequate and ineffective.

Cataloging and classification

The purpose of cataloging is to provide an index to the book collection. The card catalog, correctly organized, provides a record on cards of all books in the library. It serves as an index to the library by showing what books the library has by any given author, what books are available on any given subject, and whether a book of any given title is to be found in the library. The most useful form of card catalog for a school library is the dictionary card catalog in which cards for the author, the subject, and the title are filed together in a single alphabetical arrangement.

The purpose of classifying books is to bring all books on the same subject together on the shelves and books on related subjects near each other. The system of classification most commonly used and most desirable for school libraries is the Dewey decimal system of classification. The system was named for its founder, Melvil Dewey, a prominent figure in the library world. In the Dewey system all knowledge is divided into ten main classes numbered 000 to 900, and each class is divided into ten divisions and again into ten subdivisions. By the use of decimal points these subdivisions are divided and expanded, and thus it is possible to classify material very minutely. Abridgments must be made in this very elaborate plan in order to adapt it for use in the elementary school library. There is relatively little material on the elementary school level in many of the Dewey classification numbers. This would be true for example in such fields as library economy, philosophy, religion, economics, languages, and mathematics. The abridgment which follows is one which has been used satisfactorily in many elementary school libraries. This abridged classification is entirely adequate for most elementary school libraries. However, if a more extensive abridgment is desired, it is suggested that the "Outline of Classification" given in the *Children's Catalog*[1] be used.

ABRIDGED DEWEY DECIMAL SYSTEM OF CLASSIFICATION SUITABLE
FOR ELEMENTARY SCHOOL LIBRARIES

000	GENERAL WORKS	300	SOCIOLOGY
020	Libraries—How to Use	310	Almanacs
	Books and Libraries	320	Government
030	Encyclopedias	330	Money
100	PHILOSOPHY	351	Administration of Government. F.B.I.
170	Conduct. Etiquette.		
	Thrift	353	Citizenship
200	RELIGION	355	Army and Army Life
220	Bible Stories	359	Navy and Navy Life
290	Myths	370	Teachers' Books

[1] Ruth Giles and Dorothy E. Cook, comps., *Children's Catalog* (8th ed.; New York: H. W. Wilson, 1951).

380	Transportation. Railroads and Ships. Communication	900	HISTORY (General)
		910	Geography. Description and Travel (General)
383	Stamps	912	Atlases
391	Costumes	914	Europe (General)
394	Holidays	914.2	England
398	Fairy Tales. Legends	914.3	Germany
400	LANGUAGE	914.4	France
420	Dictionaries. Language Books	914.5	Italy
		914.6	Spain
500	SCIENCE (General)	914.7	Russia
511	Arithmetic	914.8	Scandinavia
573	Prehistoric Man	914.9	Other Countries
580	Trees	915	Asia (General)
590	Animals. Animal Stories	915.1	China
595	Insects	915.2	Japan
597	Fishes. Frogs	915.4	India
598	Birds	916	Africa
600	USEFUL ARTS—INDUSTRIES (General)	917	North America
		917.2	Mexico
608	Inventions	917.3	United States
614	Health. Fire Protection and Prevention. Safety Education	917.94	California[2]
		918	South America
		919	Oceania
621.3	Radio. Television		Philippine Islands
629	Aviation. Automobiles		Hawaiian Islands
630	Agriculture. Gardening		Australia
640	Homemaking. Cookery		New Zealand
655	Printing		South Sea Islands
680	Handicrafts	919.8	Arctic Regions
700	FINE ARTS (General)	920	Collective Biography
778	Motion Pictures	921	Individual Biography
780	Music	929	Flags
790	Games. Entertainment. Sports	930	Ancient History
		970.1	Indians
800	LITERATURE	973	United States History
810	Books about Literature	979.4	California History[2]
811	Poetry	F	Fiction
812	Plays	X	Easy Books

[2] These numbers for a particular state are inserted merely to indicate that a school may wish to use the classification numbers of a particular state in order to keep materials of local interest together.

Centralized cataloging

Centralized cataloging probably offers the most satisfactory plan for the cataloging of books in any system which involves a large number of libraries. Under this plan a central organization is set up to catalog all books which are to be placed in the various school libraries. Where school libraries are maintained by the board of education, the work is carried on as a phase of the central administration and supervision of school library service. It is ordinarily under the direction of the director or supervisor of school libraries. Where school libraries are maintained as the joint responsibility of the board of education and the city library, the cataloging is usually the responsibility of the city library. Centralized cataloging has much to commend it. It usually assures more efficient work; it makes for uniformity in cataloging in all the schools in a school system; and it relieves the busy librarian or teacher-librarian of a heavy responsibility. Cataloging and classification are time-consuming tasks, and even though the school librarian may have necessary training for the work she is quite likely to have little time to devote to it.

It is of the greatest importance that the person in charge of centralized cataloging be more than a cataloging specialist. She should be thoroughly familiar with the elementary school curriculum, the teaching procedures, and the school program as a whole. She must make certain adjustments in her cataloging on the basis of the curriculum, and yet she must not swerve too far from the standard pattern. She needs to keep in mind constantly the fact that all classification and cataloging must bear a direct relationship to the school program. She must seek to bring out through subject cards the kind of information that is required for the carrying out of the curriculum. The most appropriate list of subject headings for use in cataloging for elementary school use is *Subject Headings for Children's Materials* by Eloise Rue and Effie LaPlante.[3]

The points mentioned above are emphasized because highly trained specialists in cataloging sometimes have been employed to catalog elementary school libraries, and, although the work is perfect according to standards for cataloging, the results are impractical for the everyday needs of elementary school children and teachers.

---

[3] Eloise Rue and Effie LaPlante, *Subject Headings for Children's Materials* (Chicago: American Library Association, 1952).

Substitutes for centralized cataloging

If the school librarian has no training in cataloging, or if a school system is too small to afford centralized cataloging, some other arrangements must be made to provide for the proper organization of the library book collection. The following are plans which may be used to provide cataloging for elementary school libraries:

1. *The board of education may contract with the public library to catalog the school library.* This plan has been worked out successfully in a number of communities and is a commendable form of school and public library cooperation.

2. *The board of education may hire an experienced cataloger each year to catalog the new books.* There are situations where this plan has been used satisfactorily over a period of years. However, it often presents difficulties since it is not easy to get expert catalogers for odd jobs at odd times, especially in smaller towns and cities.

3. *Printed catalog cards may be purchased.* The H. W. Wilson Company is now printing catalog cards for a number of children's books. The classification is based on the *Children's Catalog* and the *Standard Catalog for High School Libraries.* The company provides a check list of cards available, and the cards can be purchased for a nominal sum. If Wilson-printed cards are used, a complete set of cards should be purchased for each book. The set includes author, title, and subject cards bearing subject headings and classification numbers.

Cataloging by the school librarian

There will always be schools in which the cataloging must be done by the person in charge of the library if the library is to be cataloged at all. The librarian with professional training will be able to carry on the cataloging in a satisfactory manner. The untrained person must seek expert help in undertaking the task if the results are to be authentic, practical, and usable. Fortunately, good manuals for simplified cataloging are available. The untrained and inexperienced person who attempts to catalog books should select a manual and follow instructions implicitly. Attempts to change fundamental principles which the manuals suggest invariably lead to confusion. A good manual for use in cataloging elementary school libraries is:

Douglas, Mary Peacock. *The Teacher-Librarian's Handbook.* 2d ed. Chicago: American Library Association, 1949. $2.75.

PREPARATION OF THE BOOKS FOR THE SHELVES

The initial collection

The first step in installing library service in a school is to assemble all books in the library. Such books may have been housed in the principal's office, in storerooms, or in closets, but the greatest number will be found in individual classrooms where they quite likely have come to be considered the property of the individual teachers. Teachers should understand clearly the purposes of a central library in the school. There may be some reluctance to giving up "their books" and antagonisms may actually develop, unless they understand thoroughly the aims of the library. The developing of this understanding is a task in which the principal and the librarian need to cooperate. As the organization of the library proceeds, the principal should call in from the classrooms other library materials such as maps, pictures, and other instructional aids. The aim should be to develop the library as the center for all instructional materials in the school.

All books which have been assembled must be carefully reviewed and evaluated. The principal or a teacher appointed by the principal should share with the librarian the responsibility of making decisions about books. Some books will have no permanent value and should be discarded. Such books should never be returned to the classrooms. If they are unsuitable for library use, they are also unsuitable for classroom use. Among the worth-while and useful books may be some which are in poor physical condition. These should be kept in a group together and should be repaired or rebound before they are added to the book collection of the new library.

Processing books

There are a few fundamental steps in the organization of any book collection. One process depends upon another, and if these processes or steps are carried out one by one in a systematic and thorough manner the collection will be organized in the shortest possible time. If the processing of books is done in a hit or miss fashion, much time is wasted and errors may occur which will show up only when the books are placed in circulation. Processing of the books collected in the school can begin just as soon as decisions are made upon titles which are to be kept. In order to insure wise expenditure of funds, this collection of books should be considered carefully before the initial order for new books for the library is made.

The following steps in the processing of books, carried out in order, will greatly facilitate the organization of any book collection regardless of size:

1. Classification
2. Shelf-listing
3. Mechanical preparation of the book for the shelves
     Opening the book properly
     Collating
     Making bookcard
     Pasting bookpocket and date slip in book
     Stamping name of the library in book
     Lettering
     Shellacking
4. Placing books in proper order on shelves
5. Cataloging
6. Filing shelf list and catalog cards

Where centralized cataloging is used, or where other provision is made for these processes, the school librarian will not have to consider item 1, Classification, item 2, Shelf-listing, and item 5, Cataloging. Centralized cataloging sometimes includes some of the other items listed above. However, information about all items except classification, shelf-listing, and cataloging will be given here since it will be useful to any person charged with the mechanical preparation of books for the shelves.

Mechanical preparation of the book for the shelves. Correct preparation of a book requires care, since the life of a book depends to a great extent upon the manner in which it is handled when it is new. The process is very simple when it is understood, and it is an activity in which children can assist. Practically the entire process can be carried on by committees of children working under the guidance of the librarian. Children who assist in the work must be shown the importance of neat, careful work, and untidy and shiftless work should never be tolerated. The instruction should stress the importance of neat pasting, neat stamping of books, and neat lettering and shellacking in order to get the children in the habit of careful and exact work regardless of the job at hand.

Correct mechanical preparation of books includes the following items. If the work is carried out in the order suggested below, it will be greatly facilitated.

> All books must be opened properly so that the back will not be broken. This is done by placing the back on a flat surface, opening a few pages from the front and pressing gently, then a few pages from the back of the book in the same manner. This process should be repeated with a few pages near the front, then a few pages near the back until all pages have been opened. A book treated in this manner usually will lie open easily. If there are uncut pages, they should be cut with an upward movement of a sharp knife.
>
> The entire book must be checked through to see that pages and plates are in proper order and that the book is a perfect copy. This process, called *collation,* is very important since imperfect books should be returned immediately for replacement.
>
> A bookpocket must be pasted on the inside front cover of every book which is to circulate. The lower edge of the pocket should be about one-half inch from the bottom of the cover. The purpose of the pocket is to hold the bookcard used for recording circulation. The copy number of the book is written near the top of the bookcard. Some librarians write the entire call number on the bookpocket. If a bookplate is used, the pocket can be placed on the inside back cover. Any good library paste is satisfactory, and a generous edging of paste along the open edge and dots of paste at the lower corners are sufficient. It is not necessary to put paste over the entire back of the pocket.
>
> If books are to circulate for home use, a date slip should be pasted on the flyleaf opposite the bookpocket.
>
> A bookcard with the following information,[4] either typed or handwritten, should be placed in the bookpocket: author, title, call number, and copy number.

---

[4] The information on the bookcard may vary according to the plan used for cataloging.

590 S	c. 1
Author Stearns.	
Title Sleek: the story of an otter.	
Date Due	Borrower's Name

Bookcard

A rubber stamp bearing the name of the school library in clear lettering is a necessity for marking ownership. It is advisable to stamp all books uniformly on the bookpocket, on the title page, and on one other page in the book, such as page 33.

The call number is written in the book on the flyleaf, on the title page, or on the verso of the title page when it is classified. This call number must also be lettered about one and one-half inches from the bottom of the back edge of the book. A notch may be cut on a ruler or piece of cardboard and used as a guide to insure uniformity in lettering books. Light bindings can be lettered with India ink and dark bindings in a special library white ink. Neat, legible lettering is important, and the beginner should practice lettering some old books before beginning on books which are to have a permanent place in the library. For the best results, pens made especially for lettering books should be used.

An electric stylus is excellent to use for lettering. It is available from any library supply firm. If it is used, lettering ink will not be necessary since transfer paper is especially designed to use with the stylus. A useful pamphlet on lettering books is:

American Library Association. Committee on Bookbinding. *Lettering on Library Books.* Chicago: The Association, 1919. 25c.

A coat of white shellac or book lacquer helps to preserve ink lettering on the outside cover. It helps also to keep the cover clean and adds to the life of the book. Most shellac deteriorates rapidly after the container has been opened. Special shellac containers which can be purchased from library supply houses help to take care of this difficulty, but if they are not used it is well to purchase the shellac in pints and to cover the container tightly when it is not in use. Shellac brushes can be kept clean and soft by washing them in wood alcohol after every usage. Shellacking is most successful when it is done rapidly with long swift strokes from the top of the book to the bottom. Books should be set on the edges to dry and will dry rapidly if the shellac is in good condition. Lettering done with an electric stylus does not require shellacking.

Placing books in proper order on shelves. Books are arranged on the shelves by classes in numerical order from left to right, alphabetically by the author letter, and from the top to the bottom of each section of shelving. Fiction is arranged alphabetically by the author letter. "Easy books" are kept in a special section, arranged alphabetically by author if possible. Each shelf of books is kept upright by means of a steel book support. Oversize book supports are available for large, heavy books, such as encyclopedias. When a book collection is being shelved for the first time, it is well to leave about one third of each shelf vacant to provide for future growth. Books should be pulled out to the edge of the shelves as an aid to reading titles. A shelf label with classification numbers and subjects clearly indicated should be placed in the middle of every shelf.

Filing shelf list cards

The outside of the drawers of the catalog case which contain the shelf list cards should be plainly labeled "Shelf List." Some librarians prefer to have the drawers for the shelf list separate from the card catalog and placed on the library desk where they are readily available for reference. The shelf list cards are filed in numerical order according to the classification number and then alphabetically by the author letter. This makes the shelf list a record of the books as they stand on the shelves. Guide cards with classification numbers indicated should be used to divide the cards for the different classifications.

Filing catalog cards

Since the card catalog is a dictionary catalog, all the catalog cards are filed in the catalog drawers in alphabetical order, word by word, according to the top line on each card. The outside of each drawer should have a label indicating the letters which will be found inside. Guide cards should be placed inside the drawers of the card catalog as an aid in locating cards. These should include alphabetical guides, guides with combinations of letters, and guides with subject headings. A guide card for every two or three inches of cards is not too many.

The following, simple "Rules for Filing Catalog Cards" have been worked out especially for elementary school libraries and should be carefully observed if proper instruction in library usage is to be given to classes.

RULES FOR FILING CATALOG CARDS[5]

1. Arrange Author, Subject, and Title cards together in alphabetical order. The catalog then becomes a dictionary catalog of the books in the library.
2. Disregard the initial articles "A" and "The" in titles, and begin filing with the word following the article. Within a title, these articles are to be considered as words, however.

---

[5] Sacramento City Unified School District, *Manual and Course of Study for Elementary School Libraries* (Sacramento, Calif.: Sacramento City Unified School District, September 1948), p. 17-19.

3. Arrange cards word by word, alphabetizing letter by letter, to the end of each word.

Example: Correct

New Champlin cyclopedia for young folks

NEW ENGLAND

New moon

New worlds for Josie

Newberry, Clare

Newkirk, Louis

Incorrect

Newberry, Clare

New Champlin cyclopedia for young folks

NEW ENGLAND

Newkirk, Louis

New moon

4. Arrange abbreviations or shortened words as if spelled out.

Example: Dr. as doctor

Mc as Mac

Mr. as mister

Mrs. as mistress

Mt. as mountain

N. Y. as New York

St. as Saint

U. S. as United States

5. Arrange numerals in titles of books as if spelled out. Spell numerals as they are spoken.

Example: 1 as one

101 as one hundred one (not as one hundred *and* one)

1500 as fifteen hundred, etc.

6. Arrange all books by the same author alphabetically by title.

Example: Alcott, Louisa M.

Jack and Jill.

Alcott, Louisa M.

Little men.

Alcott, Louisa M.

Little women.

7. When the same word serves for Author, Subject, and Title, arrange cards in the following order: Author cards, Subject cards, and Title cards.

Example: Homes, Alice (author)

Homes, Gerald (author)

*Children assist in preparing books
for the shelves.*

Student committees use library resources.

Homes, Warren (author)

HOMES (subject)

Homes of the birds (title)

Irish, Ronald (author)

Irish fairy tales (title)

White, Eliza O. (author)

White, William C. (author)

The white panther (title)

8. When any given subject has several subheads, arrange in alphabetical order by subhead, and under subhead by author.

Example: ANIMALS.

Parker, Bertha M.

Animals we know.

ANIMALS, ANCIENT.

Parker, Bertha M.

Animals of yesterday.

ANIMALS—CARE.

Smith, A. Croxton.

Tail waggers.

ANIMALS, EXTINCT.

Lucas, Frederic A.

Animals of the past.

ANIMALS—STORIES.

Henry, Marguerite.

The little fellow.

ANIMALS—STORIES.

Stong, Phil.

High water.

ANIMALS—STORIES.

Stong, Phil.

Honk: the moose.

9. As the distinction between main headings with subdivisions (ANI-MALS—STORIES) and inverted headings (ANIMALS, EXTINCT) is not likely to be apparent to children, it is recommended that all headings be arranged in a straight alphabetical file, disregarding the punctuation.

Example: ANIMALS.

ANIMALS, ANCIENT.

ANIMALS—CARE.

ANIMALS, EXTINCT.

ANIMALS—STORIES.

CARE AND MENDING OF BOOKS

Only minor repairs of books should be attempted by the amateur since book repairing requires real skill. Recasing and rebinding of books should never be attempted by one who has not had good instruction and training for this work. There are many good library binderies which rebind and recase books for a nominal sum. The public library is in a position to recommend reliable binderies in any given locality.

It is always well to remove books from the shelves when they are just beginning to break. The active cooperation of both teachers and children should be enlisted in the care of the book collection and in reporting books in need of attention. All users of books need to be on the lookout for loose pages, loose plates, and tears. Loose pages and plates can be tipped in with a bit of paste or liquid plastic. Tears can be mended with mending tissue or liquid plastic. Pages can be kept clean with soft art erasers. Top, bottom, and fore edges of pages can be cleaned with carpenter's sandpaper. Worn spines can be reinforced with liquid plastic or with mystic tape which is available in a variety of colors. Soiled covers can be cleaned successfully with a sponge and vinegar solution (about three parts vinegar to one part water). After books are cleaned with vinegar they must be allowed to dry thoroughly before relettering. They should be carefully shellacked after lettering, since the cleaning removes part of the sizing from the book cloth. Principals often ask teachers to assist the librarian with book mending since it involves supplementary textbooks as well as library books. Older children, too, may help if carefully supervised by a teacher or the librarian.

DISCARDING

A very important matter in the maintenance of a book collection is the intelligent discarding of obsolete materials. This is a continuing process. In the field of social studies changes are so rapid that librarians and teachers must be constantly alert to the necessity of providing children with books which present current and authentic facts about history and geography. The changes and new discoveries in science require vigilance in that field also. Children are quick to notice out-of-dateness in some subjects. The knowledge many boys have of airplanes, for instance, is often better than the librarian's, and they quite rightly reject an out-of-date book on aviation. The seventh-grade girl resents being offered a book in home economics which shows outmoded styles. Encyclopedias and atlases must be replaced often enough to insure correct information. Librarians and teachers share the responsibility of teaching children to notice copyright or publication dates of all the material they read for information.

When books are discarded from the library they should never be given to teachers for classroom use, although teachers often request them. They should be removed from the school entirely and usually they can be sold as old paper. All catalog cards should be removed from the file when books are discarded.

INVENTORY

The purpose of an inventory is to show what books actually are in the library. In elementary school libraries an inventory should be taken at least every other year. The procedure for taking the inventory is simple; books on the shelf and books in circulation are checked against the shelf list file and losses are indicated on the cards. A simple inventory sheet can be used for tabulating results. This sheet may be arranged by classification to show how many books have been lost or discarded in a single classification during the year. Books added during the year may be shown also if there is need for this information. Children become good assistants in taking inventory when properly trained and supervised.

chapter **10**

The selection, purchasing, and
organization of nonbook materials

Modern courses of study, especially in the fields of social studies and science, require up-to-date and authoritative information on a wide variety of subjects. One needs only to read some of the recent courses of study to realize that children and teachers must make use of many sources of information in addition to books. For example, extensive use is made of the excursion as a means of extending experience and of securing firsthand information about a subject. Pupils add to their knowledge of a subject through conferences with adults. These conferences may be with principal, librarian, parents, friends, "the butcher, the baker, or the candlestick maker." The interested child will consult with anyone who can give him the particular information he is seeking.

Visual aids are now well established as "audio-visual aids," and include talking motion pictures, silent motion pictures, filmstrips, film slides, radio and television programs, recordings, records, models, realia, maps, globes, flat pictures, and pamphlets and bulletins of various types. These materials are used for instructional purposes as a definite part of the teaching equipment, and in many schools the library has become the established center for the purchasing, housing, cataloging, and circulating of them. (*See* "The library—a materials center," p.6.) Many large school systems have well-organized, central audio-visual aid departments which circulate expensive equipment and materials directly to classrooms. In such situations the library usually is not involved in audio-visual services, although it may serve as a receiving and distributing center.

FUGITIVE MATERIAL

These new mediums of education have increased the demand for reading materials, and the reading materials provided must now include more than an abundant supply of books. Often the most up-to-date material on a subject is contained in newspapers, magazines, pamphlets, or bulletins rather than in books. It is important that children and teachers have such materials available to them. In order to meet the demand for this type of material, schools have organized extensive collections under such names as "Materials Bureau," "Pamphlet and Picture File," or "Fugitive File." The material often called "fugitive material"—perhaps because it is so easily lost!— must be wisely selected and carefully organized so that it can be easily located and available for classroom use. The best center for this type of material is the library. The librarian is in a good position to collect, organize, and care for such material and to set up a plan for its circulation to classrooms. The difficulty with collecting it in individual classrooms is that it is not available for use by other classes and frequently it is not well organized or kept up to date. Also, it involves a large expense if adequate equipment for housing the material is provided each classroom.

Where to collect materials

The most common types of fugitive materials are pamphlets and bulletins, clippings and excerpts, pictures, book jackets, and maps. The source of materials is almost unlimited. Pamphlets and bulletins are usually publications of the federal, state, and local government offices, of chambers of commerce, of private manufacturing companies, of railroad, steamship, and airline companies, of publishing houses, of travel bureaus, and of organizations such as the Red Cross, the American Automobile Association, and the various educational associations. Many of these publications are attractive and informative and are free from objectionable advertising. Some of the most beautiful bulletins on our national parks are issued by the railroad companies. Clippings and excerpts are obtained from magazines, newspapers, pamphlets, bulletins, and at times from discarded books. Pictures and maps can be gleaned from magazines, advertising bulletins and materials, publishers' catalogs, from oil companies, from calendars, and from discarded books. To collect this type of material is to engage in a most exciting and interesting adventure. The clever librarian will advertise the pamphlet file to all teachers and children in the school and will seek their cooperation in building up the collection. This will net much useless material plus a great deal of priceless material and a great amount of enthusiasm on the part of the future users.

The following are useful guides to the selection of pamphlets and pictures:

Vertical File Service. New York: H. W. Wilson. Sold on service basis. Write for price.

> A monthly, cumulated list of pamphlet materials. Especially useful in schools which maintain seventh and eighth grades.

Subscription Books Bulletin, October 1946. Chicago: American Library Association. 50c.

> This number, entitled *The Library's Picture Collection,* lists sources offering worth-while pictures, charts, and posters and gives evaluations of them. Reviews are grouped according to three general types of sources: commercial firms, museums and art dealers, and societies, associations, and government agencies. Lists a number of firms which issue free and very inexpensive materials.

The following magazines contain lists of inexpensive materials:

The Booklist. Chicago: American Library Association. Twice a month. $6 a year.

School Life. Washington, D. C.: Office of Education. Monthly. $1 a year.

Wilson Library Bulletin. New York: H. W. Wilson. Monthly. $2 a year.

What to collect

Great care must be used in selecting materials since it is easy to clutter the collection with useless material. Courses of study and actual use must be kept in mind. Many of the federal and state bulletins are beyond the comprehension of elementary school children, but they will be useful to teachers and for this reason should be included. The librarian must find justification for every item which she keeps. Quite as important as care in the selection of materials is the necessity for constant "weeding out" of out-of-date and useless materials. The collection will rapidly assume bulky proportions unless it is constantly being revised. Librarians may seek the help and advice of teachers on discarding materials.

Care of materials

Fugitive materials are most accessible when housed in a legal-size vertical file. All materials should be filed alphabetically by subject, according to a carefully worked-out list of subject headings. The list of subject headings should be based on local courses of study if possible. The list of subject headings on page 106 is an extensive one and is broad in its scope. Modern courses of study were kept in mind in making the list, and it can be adapted to fit almost any situation.

In arranging materials for filing, one must study each item carefully before assigning a subject heading to it. This may necessitate the reading of an entire bulletin or excerpt before making a final decision. Material should be placed where it will receive the most use. The subject headings which are used should be checked on the list of subject headings in use so that the librarian may have a record of all subjects on which material is available. The following suggestions may prove helpful in classifying and arranging materials.

Provide pressboard dividers in the vertical file. Print or type the subject headings with "See" or "See also" references on gummed tape and fold over tab of divider.

Print or type "See" references in red. Print or type "See also" references in black.

Stamp the name of the library on every piece of material.

Write the subject heading on the upper right-hand corner of every pamphlet in pencil.

Clippings, excerpts, folded maps, unmounted pictures, and book jackets can be placed in large envelopes. Write the subject heading on the upper right-hand corner of each item in the envelope and also on the envelope.

Write the subject heading *on the back* of unmounted pictures.

File all materials alphabetically by subject heading. (*See* subject headings, p.106.)

Some librarians prefer to house the picture collection separate from the pamphlet collection. Others prefer to have all the materials on one subject together. Teachers should be consulted before a decision is reached, for teachers, too, have their preferences in the matter and they are the users of the materials.

Book jackets

Book jackets represent one of the finest sources for stimulating children's interest in reading. Many of them are beautifully designed and reflect the best of an illustrator's work. They are used extensively in library publicity and often are used by the art teacher to show children fine design or artistic use of color. Because they can be used over and over, they require special care in handling. After removing a jacket from the book, one should cut off the two ends which usually contain the publisher's blurb and biographical information about the author. The blurb may be pasted in the back of the book to be referred to by children when they are browsing, or it may be pasted in a notebook advertising new books or books on a particular subject to be used by children when they are selecting a new book to read. The covers of these notebooks can be made by art classes or by a committee of pupil library assistants. These notebooks are very popular with both children and teachers. The biographical material may be filed in the vertical file under the subject heading "Authors" for future reference, or it may be used for bulletin board displays either in connection with the books or as a part of special author or illustrator displays. Sometimes the decoration on the book jacket extends across the entire jacket. In this case no cutting is necessary since the entire jacket is then used for display purposes.

Book jackets are used constantly and they need to be systematically filed so that they are readily available. The best arrangement is to file them apart from other fugitive materials, either in a separate drawer of the pamphlet file or in a large box-type file. They may be filed in large filing envelopes alphabetically by author or alphabetically by title. They may be filed according to the classification number of the books, or they may be filed according to broad subjects. Any of these systems is good if it is followed consistently.

INEXPENSIVE "BOOKS"

Within the past few years a new field of materials for children has been developing. The format is such that the material can be considered as either "books" or "pamphlets." It is all paper bound and for that reason is being discussed in this chapter on pamphlet materials. All of the material is inexpensively priced from forty cents to sixty-five cents, although for an additional charge some of it can be obtained in regular buckram or board covers. It covers a wide interest and reading range and is both factual and literary in content. Much of the factual material is written by authorities in the particular subject fields, while specialists in the field of children's literature have contributed to the story-type material. Some of the pamphlets are unusual in their illustrations and represent excellent art and color work. For the most part the print and paper are good. These materials are being published by several publishing houses.

This paper-bound material has a definite and important place in any elementary school library. It is so inexpensive that most schools can afford to purchase it and can afford, also, to replace copies freely as they become soiled and worn. It is not meant to last for years, but it fills a real need in that it presents much fine material in an inexpensive format which can be used up and replaced with newer and more up-to-date material of the same type. Also, the publishing houses which are concentrating on factual material are attempting to bring out up-to-date, authoritative material which often is not available to children in any other form.

The housing of this paper-bound material presents some problems. It can be classified as regular pamphlet material and housed in the vertical file. This plan is satisfactory for the factual material, but the story-type material, especially that for the primary grades, needs to be in sight where children can get to it easily. Although paper-covered pamphlets do not stand well on library shelves, some librarians prefer to classify this material as a regular part of the book collection and shelve it with other books on the same subject. They contend that although it may wear out more quickly, its added use justifies this plan of handling. Some librarians place the material in pamphlet boxes, label the boxes with the suitable subject heading, and place the boxes on the shelves with books on the same subject. None of these plans is entirely satisfactory. The problem exists wherever the material is used, and librarians are experimenting with ways of solving it satisfactorily.

Some of the most useful material of this kind is listed below. Most of it is described and evaluated in the book lists on page 73.

Encyclopaedia Britannica Picture Stories. *World's Children Series.* 12 volumes. Chicago: Encyclopaedia Britannica Pr., 1947. 50c each.

Photographic picture books, with text by Elizabeth Solem, based on the films made by Encyclopaedia Britannica Films. Typical titles are *Mateo and the Mexican Fair, Hans of the Swiss Alps,* and *Pauli and His Hawaiian Feast.*

Junior Life Adjustment Booklets. Chicago: Science Research Associates. 40c each. Published monthly, September through May, with the subscription price of $3.50 a year, but individual copies available for purchase.

Planned especially for children in grades six through nine, and designed to help them see and solve their problems. Typical titles are *Clubs Are Fun, Exploring Atomic Energy, How You Grow,* and *You and Your Problems.*

Osswald, Edith. *Our Animal Story Books.* Boston: Heath. 40c each. A group of ten short books for children of the primary grades. Children and animals are featured through interesting stories. Large, colored pictures. Typical titles are *Peanuts the Pony, Little White Rabbit,* and *Fun for Fidelia.*

Unitexts. Evanston, Ill.: Row Peterson, 36c to 96c each.

Particularly useful for science and social studies. Beautifully illustrated in color and in black and white. Many contain colored photographs. Unitexts consist of the following series:

Basic Science Education Series. 36c to 48c each. Grades 1-9.

Basic Social Education Series. 40c each. Grades 5-9.

Film Story Books. 48c each. Grades 5-8.

Good Neighbor Series: Latin America. 64c each. Grades 7-12.

Our Freedom Series: Democracy. 64c each. Grades 7-12.

Real People Series. 48c each. Grades 5-9.

The Way of Life Series. 96c each. Grades 7-12.

Witty, Paul. *It's Fun to Find Out: Film Story Books.* Boston: Heath. 32c each.

Simply written stories which give interesting and accurate information about various ways of living. Illustrated from the sound motion pictures of the same name by Encyclopaedia Britannica Films. Typical titles are *Shep, the Farm Dog, The Fireman,* and *Gray Squirrel.*

SUGGESTED SUBJECT HEADINGS FOR FUGITIVE MATERIALS
IN ELEMENTARY SCHOOL LIBRARIES

Africa

Agriculture, *see* Farming & farm equipment

Airplanes & airways

See also: Communication (General)

Transportation (General)

Alaska
  See also: North America (General)
Animals
  See also: Birds
        Conservation (General)
        Insects
        Prehistoric animals
        Reptiles
  (subhead with name of animal if necessary)
Arbor Day
  See also: Trees
Architecture, *see* Famous buildings & monuments
                Housing
Arctic regions
Argentina
  See also: South America (General)
Armistice Day
Army & navy
Art, *see* Paintings
        Sculpture
Artists
  See also: Book illustrators & illustrations
        Famous persons
Asia (General)
  See also names of individual countries, as:
                China
                Holy Land
                India
                Japan
Australia
Authors
  See also: Famous persons

Automobiles & automobile industry
  See also: Communication (General)
        Highways
        Transportation (General)
Aviation, *see* Airplanes & airways
Belgium
  See also: Europe (General)
Bibliographies
Birds
  See also: Conservation (General)
Book illustrators & illustrations
Book jackets
Book Week
Brazil
  See also: South America (General)
Bridges
British Isles (General)
  See also: Europe (General)
  (subhead with name of country if necessary)
California (General)[1]
  See also name of particular industry
  See also: National parks & monuments (General)
        Recreation
        United States (General)
  subhead: Cities
        History
        Industries
        Recreation
        Spanish culture

---

[1] This heading for a particular state is inserted as typical of what a school would do in the organization of materials of local interest.

Canada
  See also: North America (General)
Canals
  (subhead with name of canal if necessary)
Canning & preserving industry
  See also: Foods (General)
            Refrigeration (General)
            Vegetables
Cattle raising, *see* Meat industry
Central America
  See also: North America (General)
Children of other lands
Chile
  See also: South America (General)
China
  See also: Asia (General)
Christmas
Circus
Cliff dwellers & cliff dwellings
Clothing industry
  See also: Cotton
            Flax & linen
            Furs & fur industry
            Leather
            Precious stones & jewels
            Rubber
            Silk
            Synthetics
            Wool
Clouds
Clubs & organizations
  See also: Recreation

Coal, *see* Minerals & mining
            Power—Coal
Columbus Day
  See also: Famous persons
Communication (General)
  See also: Airplanes & airways
            Automobiles & automobile industry
            Highways
            Postal service
            Publishing industry
            Railways
            Ships & shipping
            Transportation (General)
  subhead: Wire systems[2]
            Wireless systems[3]
Conservation (General)
  See also: Animals
            Birds
            Fish & fishing
            Forests & forestry
            National parks & monuments (General)
Constitution Day
Copper, *see* Minerals & mining
Costumes
Cotton
  See also: Clothing industry
Cuba
  See also: Islands (General)
Dairying
  See also: Foods—Milk
Dams
  (subhead with name of dam if necessary)
Deserts
Easter

---

[2] Includes: Telegraph, Teletypewriting, Cable, Television, Telephotography.
[3] Includes: Wireless telegraphy, Radio, Transoceanic telephone, Radiotelevision.

France
    See also: Europe (General)
Fruits & fruit industry
    See also: Farming & farm
        equipment
            Foods—Tropical fruits
Furs & fur industry
    See also: Clothing industry
Germany
    See also: Europe (General)
Geysers
Glaciers & icebergs
Glass
Gold, *see* Minerals & mining
Government (General)
Greece
    See also: Europe (General)
Hallowe'en
Handicrafts
Hawaiian Islands
    See also: Islands (General)
            South Seas
Health
    See also: Safety
Heat & heating systems
Highways
    See also: Automobiles & auto-
        mobile industry
            Communication
            (General)
            Transportation
            (General)
Hobbies
    See also: Recreation
Holidays, *see* name of particular
    holiday
Holy Land
    See also: Asia (General)
Housing
    See also: Famous buildings &
            monuments
Icebergs, *see* Glaciers & icebergs

Imports (General)
    See also: Foods (General)
            Rubber
            Silk
            Wool
India
    See also: Asia (General)
Indians
Industries (General)
    See also name of particular in-
        dustry
Insects
Inventors
    See also: Famous persons
Iron, *see* Minerals & mining
Islands (General)
    See also name of particular
        island
    See also: South Seas
Italy
    See also: Europe (General)
Japan
    See also: Asia (General)
            Silk
Labor
Labor Day
Leather
    See also: Clothing industry
            Industries (General)
Libraries
Lighthouses
Lightning
Linen, *see* Flax & linen
Lumbering
    See also: Forests & forestry
            Trees
Manufacturing (General)
Maps
Meat industry
    See also: Foods (General)
            Refrigeration
            (General)

Mediterranean countries, *see*
    Greece
    Holy Land
    Italy
    Portugal
    Spain
Memorial Day
Mexico
  See also: North America
      (General)
Minerals & mining
  See also: Precious stones & jewels
Moon, *see* Solar system
Mother's Day
Motion picture industry
Mountains
Music
Musicians
  See also: Famous persons
National forests, *see* National parks and monuments (General)
National parks and monuments (General)
  See also: Conservation
      (General)
      Recreation
      Trees
  subhead:[4] Carlsbad Caverns
      Crater Lake
      Grand Canyon
      Yellowstone
Netherlands
  See also: Europe (General)
North America (General)
  See also: Alaska
      Canada

      Central America
      Mexico
      United States
Occupations (General)
  See also name of particular occupation
  See also: Professions
      Public Service
Ocean
Oil, *see* Power—Oil
Paintings
Panama
Pan-American Day
Paper making
Peru
  See also: South America
      (General)
Philippine Islands
  See also: Islands (General)
Plays and programs
Poetry
Polar regions, *see* Arctic regions
Portugal
  See also: Europe (General)
Postal service
  See also: Communication
      (General)
Power
  subhead: Coal
      Electric
      Oil
      Water
Precious stones & jewels
  See also: Clothing industry
      Minerals & mining
Prehistoric animals
Professions
  See also: Occupations
      Public service

---

[4] Examples selected only to show alphabetical arrangement of subheads used.

Public service[5]
See also: Fire protection
Occupations
Professions
Safety
Publishing industry
See also: Communication
(General)
Radio, see Communication—
Wireless systems
Railways
See also: Communication
(General)
Refrigeration
(General)
Transportation
(General)
Recreation[6]
See also: Clubs & organizations
Hobbies
National parks & mon-
uments (General)
Refrigeration (General)
See also: Canning & preserving
Fish & fishing
Meat industry
Railways
Vegetables
Reptiles
Rocks, see Minerals & mining
Rubber
See also: Imports (General)
Russia
See also: Europe (General)
Scandinavian
countries
Safety
See also: Fire protection
Health
Public service

Scandinavian countries
See also: Europe (General)
Russia
Schools
Science (General)
Sculpture
Sea life
Seasons (General)
subhead: Autumn
Spring
Summer
Winter
Ship building
Ships & shipping
See also: Communication
(General)
Transportation
(General)
Silk
See also: Clothing industry
Imports (General)
Japan
Soap
Solar system
South America (General)
See also names of individual
countries, as:
Argentina
Brazil
Chile
Peru
South Seas
See also: Hawaiian Islands
Islands (General)
Spain
See also: Europe (General)
Stars and planets, see Solar system
Steel, see Housing
Minerals & mining
Stock raising, see Meat industry

[5] Includes: Policemen, Firemen, Garbage men, Traffic officers, etc.
[6] Includes: All types of sports, Gardening, Outdoor life, Vacationing, etc.

Stone, *see* Precious stones & jewels

Sun, *see* Solar system

Switzerland
   See also: Europe (General)

Synthetics
   See also: Clothing industry

Thanksgiving

Toys

Transportation (General)
   See also: Airplanes & airways
             Automobiles & automobile industry
             Communication (General)
             Foods (General)
             Highways
             Railways
             Ships & shipping

Trees
   See also: Forests & forestry
             Lumbering
             National parks & monuments (General)

United States (General)
   See also names of individual states
   See also: North America (General)

subhead: Civil war period
          Colonial times
          Frontier life
          Possessions, *see*
             Alaska
             Cuba
             Hawaiian Islands
             Panama
             Philippine Islands
             South Seas
          Revolutionary war period
          The Southwest
          Westward expansion

Valentine's Day

Vegetables
   See also: Farming & farm equipment
             Canning & preserving industry
             Refrigeration (General)

Volcanoes

Water & Water Power, *see* Power—Water

Weaving, *see* Clothing industry

Wool
   See also: Clothing industry
             Imports (General)

AUDIO-VISUAL AIDS

If the library is a true materials center or resource center, the librarian will be responsible for the selection of all types of audio-visual aids as well as for the cataloging, housing, and utilization of them. In the case of films, she will need to know not only where to purchase but also where to borrow them since films are very costly items. Very often state departments of education, the extension division of the state university, county and municipal school film libraries, and local public library film libraries serve as agencies for the rental of educational films. Catalogs can be obtained by writing to the agency involved. The Visual Education Service, U. S. Office of Education, Washington, D. C., offers many services to schools which are not being performed by other educational institutions or organizations. A list of publications and a description of services rendered are available upon request.

Two good guides for *films* are:

A Directory of 2002 Sixteen Millimeter Film Libraries. Washington, D. C.: Superintendent of Documents, Government Printing Office, 1952. 30c.

> Includes the names and addresses of film centers all over the United States which maintain 16-millimeter films for rental. Annotated.

Educational Film Guide, compiled by Frederic A. Krahm. New York: H. W. Wilson. Write for price.

> An annual list of 16-millimeter films, with quarterly supplements. Annotations indicate content of film and the type of group which would find it useful. Gives purchase price and rental source.

Many films suitable for school use are available free. Two guides to free films are:

Educator's Guide to Free Films. Randolph, Wis.: Educator's Progress Service. Issued annually. $6.

Notarius, Nanette. *The Handbook of Free Films.* New York: Allanan Associates, 1952. $10.

Filmstrips are less expensive than films and are usually one of the first visual-aids to be purchased by a school library. They are especially popular in elementary schools. Two guides to selection are:

Falconer, Vera. *Filmstrips.* New York: McGraw-Hill, 1948. $5.

> A comprehensive book on the subject. Gives detailed descriptions of releases through 1947. Includes a complete distributor directory.

Filmstrip Guide, compiled by Frederic A. Krahm. New York: H. W. Wilson. $8.50 a year.

> Similar in purpose and arrangement to *Educational Film Guide.*

Slides are not easy to select because there is not yet a selected list available giving recommendations from the various producers. Two important sources which issue free catalogs are:

Keystone View Company, Meadville, Pa.

> Largest producer of standard lantern slides.

Society for Visual Education, Inc., 1345 W. Diversey Parkway, Chicago 14, Ill.

> A leading producer of 2 x 2-inch slides.

There are several good guides to the selection of *records* and *transcriptions*. The following are recommended:

American Library Association, 50 East Huron Street, Chicago, Ill.
Thorne-Thomsen storytelling records. Write for catalog.
Barbour, Harriet. *The Children's Record Book*. New York: Crown Publishers, 1948. $2.40.
An authoritative guide to the best recorded music for children, classified according to age and interest.
Enrichment Records. 246 Fifth Ave., New York 1, N. Y.
Based on the true-to-history, popular Landmark Books published by Random House.
Fox Records for Children. 1558 North Vine Street, Hollywood, Calif.
Stories for children told by Martha Blair Fox. Write for free catalog.
Gloria Chandler Recordings. 277 W. 12th Street, New York 14, N. Y.
Transcriptions of the "Books Bring Adventure" radio programs. Write for free catalog.
Leavitt, Helen S. *Recordings for the Elementary School*. New York: Crown Publishers, 1949. $2.40.
Records and recordings are graded and classified by subject areas.

Additional aids to selection will be found in *Aids in Selection of Materials: Books, Films, Records, for Children and Young People*, described on page 69.

Realia can be obtained from so many sources that it is impossible to mention special companies or stores. The dime store should not be overlooked, however, as a good source.

Information about *radio and television programs* changes rapidly. Local newspapers are the best sources for obtaining information about the network programs carried by local stations and also about special programs on local stations. Some stations offer transcriptions of educational programs free to schools. Two reliable sources of network information are:

FREC List of Selected Radio and TV Network Programs, issued by the Federal Radio Education Committee of the United States Office of Education, Washington, D. C.
A listing of selected radio and TV programs selected on a broad educational basis involving educational significance, program quality, and instructional adaptability. Short descriptions of the programs with grade levels indicated. Gives network and eastern standard time. Issued twice a year. Write for free list.

Listenables and Lookables. 61 Lafayette Ave., East Orange, N. J. $2.50 a year.

> A bulletin issued three times a month, except during the summer months. Gives information about both radio and TV network programs, with eastern standard time. Sometimes describes the programs and gives techniques for utilization in the classroom. Always gives advance news concerning new programs about to appear.

Kinescope recordings of TV programs offer a new source for films. Some of the popular children's book programs from "Telaventure Tales" (*see* p.8) have been released on kinescope recordings. Information on these films can be obtained from *Gloria Chandler Records,* 277 W. 12th Street, New York 14, N. Y.

The librarian who must process and catalog audio-visual materials should consider using the catalog cards for motion pictures and filmstrips which are printed and sold by the Library of Congress. These printed cards are a great timesaver and provide all the essential information needed about a film. The information even includes the running time and a content summary. Information can be obtained from Card Division, Library of Congress, Washington, D. C.

Additional help for organizing audio-visual aids will be found in the following publications:

Douglas, Mary Peacock. *The Teacher-Librarian's Handbook.* 2d ed. Chicago: American Library Association, 1949. $2.75.

Rufsvold, Margaret I. *Audio-Visual School Library Service.* Chicago: American Library Association, 1949. $2.75.

chapter 11

Reading guidance and

library activities

Reading is one of the finest leisure activities, but the greatest values come from reading only when one knows what to read. While the classroom teacher may teach children the mechanics of reading, actual skill in reading will come about only if children are afforded continuous opportunity to practice the art of reading. The librarian's most important task is to see that children get the right books to read at the right time. The term *right books,* in this connection, means books with content suitable to the particular child's interest and with a vocabulary suited to his reading ability. The recreational reading period in the library will serve its purpose of "recreating" only if the child is reading the "right" book for him. The help the librarian offers children and the guidance she gives them contribute to the development of satisfactory attitudes toward books and of desirable reading habits and tastes.

In guiding children's reading, it is essential to have the child feel that he is the one who makes the final choice of what he is to read. A good plan is to select two or three books from the shelves and look them over with the child. Care should be exercised to select books which are not too long or too difficult to be read with ease. This point is not so important if the child is an average or good reader, but it is very important if he is a slow or poor reader. When a child reads his first "whole" book, he gains confidence in himself and gradually he will select longer and more difficult material to read. In discussing books with children, the librarian may sketch briefly something about the books or tell an interesting incident or two from them. As she talks, she should avoid "talking down" and sweet sentimentalities. Children readily sense this type of insincerity. Always the librarian should recognize the child's point of view about books and never try to force her selections on him.

Knowing the children

There are a few fundamental principles which govern successful reading guidance. The first principle is that all effective guidance must begin with knowing the children. This requires a genuine interest in children and a sympathetic understanding of them and their problems. It involves studying the children's interests, their aptitudes, and their hobbies. It includes a study of their personalities and their reactions in different situations. It may require consultation with teachers or principals about the children. The librarian should know the reading ability of every child accurately enough to assist him in selecting materials which he can read. The librarian must accept the child's initial interests without criticism and build upon these interests, since interest in reading is a highly individual matter. Many children have an interest in books and a wide background of firsthand experience because of a good home or community environment. Other children have had little acquaintance with books and have a very meager background of experiences. Dora Smith has summed up this situation very well by stating: "The reading interests with which pupils come to school are our opportunity, but the reading interests with which they leave school are our responsibility."[1] The librarian's task is to try to analyze skillfully the background, the interests, and the needs of each individual and to try to supply him with suitable library materials. She can find help in understanding any group of children by studying research studies which have been published about interests of the various age levels as a basis for the study of her groups and of individual children within her groups.

The slow-reading child, the reluctant reader, requires careful

[1] Dora V. Smith, "Current Issues Relating to Development of Reading Interests and Tastes," *Recent Trends in Reading,* Supplementary Education Monograph No. 49 (Chicago: Univ. of Chicago Pr., 1939), p.300.

study and real patience. The librarian, through use of every psychological principle she knows, must first win over his personality and gain his complete confidence. She must try to arouse his curiosity about books and stimulate any glimmer of interest which she uncovers. She needs to be sure that the book collection offers a variety of suitable materials for these children. Books which are simply written but mature in content and "thin" books with large type and profuse illustrations are the first to appeal to the slow reader.

The gifted child needs the librarian's help, also. In many school situations, the library with its fine collection of materials offers the only outlet for the gifted child's abilities and interests. Most gifted children will do a wide variety of reading without any special encouragement, but some will not. Suitable books for children of all ages and abilities are available, and the librarian and teacher share the responsibility of making them available to the gifted child who has difficulty in finding them for himself. The gifted child often prefers books which are written for older children or for adults, and this preference is only natural. His preferences are determined by his interests and hobbies, and he should be encouraged without being led into literature beyond his maturity.

The librarian may be the first to notice, however, that preoccupation with books is depriving the gifted child of normal social development and that he is preferring solitude to companionship. He needs outdoor exercise and activities which bring him in constant contact with other children of his own age. He needs the contacts which groups such as the Boy Scouts (or Campfire Girls) can give him. He needs to take an active part in school committees or service clubs. The librarian, aware of his reading interests, is in a good position to help him broaden those interests into active participation in suitable group activities. He must learn to understand other people and how to live with them successfully and happily if he is to succeed.

Knowing the book collection

Another principle of successful reading guidance is that the librarian should have a thorough knowledge of the book collection with which she works. College courses in children's literature will be helpful only insofar as they provide for wide reading and judging of all types of children's books. The librarian should read constantly in the book collection of the library. No activity on her part will reap richer rewards. The more books she can know personally, the more effective her reading guidance becomes and the more confidence the children will have in her suggestions. Recommending books without some firsthand knowledge of them is at best a hazardous undertaking. The child is quick to lose faith in the judgment of an adult, but he is just as ready to respect and honor judgment which proves worth while to him. Lucky is the librarian who can get a child to exclaim admiringly, "Gee, you know a lot of swell books." One of the essentials of interesting children in books comes as an outgrowth of the librarian's own personal enthusiasm for books and reading.

Browsing

Another principle of reading guidance is recognition of the fact that browsing plays as important a part in children's reading as in the reading of adults. Children like to browse in books and they should be given plenty of time to do so. Choosing their own books to read is one of the greatest pleasures they experience in the library and it is one of the best ways to become acquainted with books. They need some guidance in browsing, however, so that it does not become a time-consuming activity consisting of nothing more than pulling books off the shelves for a hasty turning of pages. The librarian can help children to browse more intelligently by offering a few simple suggestions, such as the following:

Look at the author's name to see if he is a familiar author.

Look at the name of the illustrator to see if he is one you know about. Look at some of the pictures to see if they interest you.

Read any reviews or descriptions of the book which may be pasted on the inside of the cover.

If you are browsing in a book on aviation, radio, science, or social studies, notice the date of publication. It is important that such information be up to date.

Read through the table of contents or the chapter headings to get an idea of what the book is about.

Read a few paragraphs here and there in the book. This will help you to find out if the book is easy for you to read and will also give you an idea of the author's style.

After the librarian has made suggestions to the children, she should leave them alone to enjoy a pleasurable and informal association with books. She will naturally "keep an eye on" the books the individual children select to read, since this is the best way for her to gain an understanding of their particular interests. There may be times when a child does not select a book to read as a result of his browsing. That, too, is legitimate. He may be reading a bit from this book and a bit from that book, gleaning information and thoroughly enjoying himself, yet he does not feel that he wants to choose a book to read. Sometimes when a child has just finished a long book, he is not quite in the mood to start another book and will, therefore, indulge in considerable browsing. The clever librarian will find many ways to assist the child who seems unable to settle down to substantial reading after browsing about for a reasonable time.

Bibliotherapy

Reading guidance includes the application of bibliotherapy, especially for emotionally disturbed children who are problems. It can become a positive factor in helping children with their personality adjustments and in the development of wholesome ideals and basic principles of conduct. Good rapport between the librarian and the child is essential, and the use of bibliotherapy presupposes a thorough understanding on the part of the librarian of the book collection with which she works. Excellent suggestions for this phase of reading guidance are contained in *Character Formation Through Books* by Clara Kircher,[2] *Reading Ladders for Human Relations* by the American Council on Education,[3] and *Growing with Books* by Bernice Leary.[4] Lists of books in these publications are organized according to the ideas or character traits which the books illustrate. The assumption is that by reading the books the child will identify himself with the book character who faces a problem or a situation similar to his own. It is hoped that by this identification the child's attitudes and behavior will be influenced so that he may adjust to his own situation. The total reading pro-

[2] Clara J. Kircher, comp., *Character Formation Through Books* (rev. ed.; Washington, D. C.: Catholic Univ. of America Pr., 1952).
[3] American Council on Education, *Reading Ladders for Human Relations* (rev. and enl. ed.; Washington, D. C.: The Council, 1949).
[4] Bernice Leary, *Growing with Books: A Reading Guide* (1952-53 ed.; Eau Claire, Wis.: E. M. Hale, 1952).

gram of any school can be considered "good" only when it creates a real desire on the part of children to read, a desire to seek books not only for pleasure and for information but also for personal help and development.

LIBRARY ACTIVITIES

The effectiveness of the library in carrying out its varied functions depends upon many factors. The importance and interrelationship of physical setup, personnel, materials, and reading guidance have already been discussed. Quite as important as any of these factors, however, is the program of library activities. The relation of the teacher to the library program is fully discussed in "The teacher cooperating with the library," page 25, and it must be kept in mind that the classroom provides the real basis for the functional use of the library. However, many beginning librarians faced with a library program which includes the daily scheduling of classes to the library ask worriedly, "But what shall I do with the children every day? Shall I plan something definite for each period or just let them read?" A regular, planned program seems to be the best solution to the problem. Successful programs now in operation include recreational reading, sharing reading experiences, instruction in library usage, and reference work in connection with classroom assignments. Any program must be kept flexible, but the librarian will find that good results can be accomplished by arranging a program for each class which will include these activities every week. Discussions of the activities appear in succeeding chapters.

chapter 12

Recreational reading

The teaching of literature should mean, at the beginning, reading of worth-while books to little children who can't read. Without false sentiment, it may be said that most people carry as their chief literary asset the remembrance of "What mother read aloud to them when they were kids." But then "mother" never held exams, or asked the children to name the six chief sages to Old Mother Hubbard and the Snow Queen. The reading was for reading's sake, and it led the child into the magic garden to which presently, able to read, he could resort of himself; out of the garden the school-teacher afterwards chased him with a written exam.—Too Much College, by Stephen Leacock.

The term *recreational reading* refers to the type of reading which the child does for the sheer fun of reading. It is reading which brings enjoyment. It is reading which carries with it adventure into new worlds. It is reading which entertains, delights, and recreates. Such reading is sometimes referred to as *free reading*—"free" because the child is free to read whatever interests and entertains him without any restrictions. This reading may be fiction or non-fiction. It may be from magazines, from an encyclopedia, or from pamphlets. Because the reading is free or recreational, there is no reason to believe that all such reading is light and merely a "time filler." A difficult book on electricity may be recreation for some boy who spends time working on electrical contrivances. A book of fairy tales may be recreation for some imaginative youngster. A factual book in social studies may be recreation for the child who has been privileged to travel a great deal. A guidebook about birds or trees may be recreation for children who love the out-of-doors. A class engaged in recreational reading is a living picture of individual differences. It depicts the wants, hopes, dreams, interests, ideas, and ideals of the children. As the child reads, his horizon is widening, his spirit is deepening, he is becoming more aware of other peoples and places, his imagination is stirred, and his emotional experiences are constantly enriched.

Children who have had the privilege of becoming acquainted with books in the home know by the time they enter kindergarten that books may be looked to as a source of amusement, adventure, excitement, and information. These are the children who grow up knowing Mother Goose, who know the happy childhood verses of Robert Louis Stevenson, who look upon Winnie the Pooh as a personal friend, and who can substitute the correct word in many a passage from *Peter Rabbit, Little Black Sambo,* or fairy tales of Andersen and the brothers Grimm. Reading has always meant recreation for them, although the actual reading has been done by some adult and the child has had the role of listener. For the hordes of children who enter school with a limited background of first-hand experiences and no book experiences at all, books may have little or no meaning. It becomes the responsibility of the school to supply these children with the knowledge and realization that books are great sources of fun, of adventure, and of excitement as well as useful sources of information.

Factors which affect reading

Reading is affected by many factors. It is important to keep these in mind in planning any program of recreational reading in the school. Some of the more important of these factors are:

A well-selected collection of books, balanced as to subject fields and reading levels

A comfortable and attractive environment conducive to reading

An atmosphere of informality and freedom in the library

Wise and subtle guidance in reading at the time it is needed

Bulletin board displays and exhibits in the library carefully planned to encourage reading

Provision for daily access to the library giving repeated opportunities to read

All books and other materials properly organized so that they are easily accessible for use by children

The school which provides well for the above factors will find that the recreational reading program will almost carry itself. A class comes to the library for free reading. Many of the children will go directly to the shelves to get the particular books they want to read. Others may browse about a few moments, finally select something, and settle down to read. Others may browse about for a longer period, some of them selecting books and others being unable to find anything which pleases. Some children will voluntarily seek the help of the librarian; others the librarian will need to assist in such a subtle manner that they still feel they have selected their own books. After a child has selected a book to read, it is important that he be left alone to read in peace. The librarian no longer has any place in the picture. The child and the book need to make each other's acquaintance, and they can do it best if left alone. There can be no more delightful period in the school day for children than the recreational reading period if the children are given the freedom to enjoy it to the full.

Testing recreational reading

A question often raised with regard to the recreational reading program is whether or not to set up a testing program for the testing of reading results. The difficulty with any plan for the testing of recreational reading is that it removes freedom from the reading and tends to defeat the aims of such reading. "How can we be sure the child is understanding what he is reading unless we have some sort of checkup?" is the question sometimes asked. The best answer may be another question: "Is not the fact that the child sits quietly and reads for twenty or thirty minutes conclusive evidence that he is understanding what he is reading?" Even the fact that he may become weary and restless during the period does not always mean that he is *not* understanding what he reads. It may mean that he is not interested in the particular book he is reading. The solution of the problem lies in giving the child the opportunity to choose a book which interests him and which presents no serious vocabulary or reading difficulties to him. Then and only then will his reading become recreational. There is no adequate measure of an individual's personal enjoyment of anything. How can we test what a child gets from what he reads for pleasure? He alone must judge of what pleases him and of what has meaning to him. These values are immeasurable. Schools should forget all about testing recreational reading and confine testing to the periods set aside for the teaching of reading. Let librarians devote time and thought to selecting the finest books available. Let them give children freedom and time to read. Let them do all in their power to see that children and books are brought together in a happy relationship. Soon the schools will realize that there is no need for the testing of free or recreational reading.

There may be no harm in making informal use of tests where children use them to judge their own reading. Children are like adults in many ways. Many adults enjoy taking the reading tests which appear in some of the leading magazines. They take such tests "for fun." They always enjoy checking up on themselves with the answer page after they find out their scores. They may form some judgment of their own ability, but they know very well that no one else is going to have the chance to judge them by their score. Children like to test themselves in this same way. Some librarians make up true-false or multiple choice tests for popular children's books, with correct answer cards. When these tests are used with children, they should be used in the very same way that adults make use of the reading tests mentioned. The children take them only if they wish to take them. They score themselves by using the answer card. They may or may not discuss their score with the librarian, although it is quite interesting to note that when children do take these tests they almost always show the librarian how they have come out with the answers. The children know that the librarian is not judging them or their reading by their scores on the tests. They know, however, that she is interested in their reading and their accomplishments. The whole procedure is an informal one.

Closely related to the question of testing recreational reading is the question of whether or not grades or marks should be given for library reading or other library activities. The giving of marks in this connection appears to be a very objectionable practice. It tends to destroy children's freedom to use the library in a truly recreational sense; it forces children who are slow readers to associate the library with unhappy reading experiences; and it tends to formalize the library program. Furthermore, many of the activities do not lend themselves to satisfactory evaluation in terms of grades or marks.

Individual reading records

There is much difference of opinion about the value of keeping a record of children's reading. Most librarians agree that there is no place in the library program for the kind of reading record or reading chart which shows the extent of one child's reading as compared with that of another child. There are many who believe that there is a place for an individual record kept by each child of the reading he does year by year. Such records usually list author, title, type of book, date book was started, and date book was completed. This type of record is a means of watching the child's development in reading. It shows his interests. It helps the librarian to expand the child's interests by leading him quite naturally from the type of book he reads continuously to other books in related fields. Many children take pride in the records of what they have read and enjoy taking the records home to parents at the end of the year. The librarian must be sure that children understand thoroughly that this record is nothing more than a means of helping them to remember what books they have read each year. There must be no premium placed on it so that children feel they have reason to pad their record. There should never be comparisons between the individual reading records of children. The shortest list often represents the most fruitful reading. If a reading record is kept, it should be simple in form, it should not involve a great deal of effort on the part of either the children or the librarian to maintain, and it should be in a form that is easy to file.

chapter **13**

Sharing reading

experiences

Part of the fun children get from reading comes from discussing with others what they have read. The library program should afford children plenty of opportunity to share their reading experiences with one another. The two principal ways in which children may share their reading experiences are through group discussions of books, authors, and illustrators, and through storytelling and reading aloud.

Group discussions

One of the purposes of the elementary school library is to develop in children a lasting interest in reading for pleasure as well as for information. There are some educational leaders who believe that this function can be carried out successfully by exposing children to the very best books and then giving them continuous opportunities to read unmolested to their hearts' content. There are others who believe, however, that children will gain more pleasure from books if they know more about them—their authors, their illustrators, and their artistic qualities. We seek to heighten the child's appreciation of books and reading because we as adults believe that an appreciation of the best in literature, art, music, and the sciences enriches living, furnishes growing interests for leisure hours, and makes for more interesting and integrated personalities. Reading

Let's pretend.

*Tape recordings bring
new stories.*

broadens the child's horizon in the same way that it broadens the adult's. It is entirely possible that group discussions about authors, illustrators, and beautiful books will open new worlds to children, will assist in the refinement of reading tastes, and will increase the power of discrimination in reading choices. Group discussions should not be thought of as a way to teach appreciation. Appreciation probably cannot be taught, but it can be and often is "caught."

Many children need help in expressing their ideas about books. To say that a book is "interesting," "swell," or "the best I've ever read" means little. An excellent chapter in *The Children's Book on How to Use Books and Libraries*,[1] entitled "When You Tell Other People about Books," may be used as an introduction to group discussions. Children enjoy learning the words suggested in the chapter for describing books and offer additional descriptive words which they soon begin to use with facility. In all group discussions, freedom of expression should be encouraged. Children should feel as free to tell why they do not like a particular book as why they like it. They should be made to feel that their opinions are important but not final. General participation must be encouraged so that the discussion is not carried on by only a few of the more aggressive children. The more retiring child often has very interesting reactions to his reading, but he is shy about expressing himself. The librarian's task is to assist every child to become a contributing member of the group, in terms of his own abilities. Group discussions give fine opportunity for developing good listening practices and thoughtful evaluations. They bring out original ideas on many subjects and stimulate real thinking about what has been read.

The discussions should be informal with the children grouped about in such a way that talking together is natural and easy. Tables can be pushed back and chairs grouped in a small circle. An atmosphere of formality or of the stage being set for the activity will interfere with the success of it. These group discussions offer the finest opportunities it is possible to have to develop in children definite standards for judging books. While children cannot appreciate abstract literary criticism, they can understand such concrete things as whether or not a book was interesting, whether the char-

---

[1] Carolyn Mott and Leo B. Baisden, *The Children's Book on How to Use Books and Libraries* (New York: Scribner, 1948).

acters seemed true to life, or whether something new was learned from the book. They have their own ideas and need the opportunity to express them. Given the opportunity they soon discover that a book shared is doubly enjoyed.

Suggestions for group discussions

The following suggestions for group discussions can be adapted for use with any grade. From the time children begin to handle books they can learn to appreciate their beauty and value.

Discussions about beautiful books. Show different editions of the same title and note the illustrations, paper, print, and binding of each. Try to get the children to notice the difference in these points as it affects the beauty of the book.

Discuss the values of school editions for popular books.

Emphasize the importance of the illustrator in the making of a book.

Arrange a display of beautifully illustrated books. Let the children select a few favorites which they wish to know more about. Show them the front cover and then the back cover, noting all the artistic details. Show the end leaves if they are decorated. Spend some time discussing the title page, emphasizing its beauty as well as the important information it contains. Discuss the dedication, if there is one, and read the preface. Next note the illustrations. Note the use of color, black-and-white line sketches, or silhouettes, as the case may be. Encourage the children to offer opinions about the illustrations. Make use of such terms as *headpieces, tailpieces, insets, full-page* and *half-page illustrations, double spreads,* and *marginal decorations.* Children like to become acquainted with these new terms. Gradually they begin to see book illustration as an art, and their contributions to the discussion show a deepening appreciation of the beautiful in books.

Discussions about illustrators. Let the children assemble and make a display of all the books in the library illustrated by one particular illustrator.

Arrange the bulletin board display about the illustrator selected.

Discuss the characteristics of his pictures. The children will be able to detect many interesting qualities.

Let the children find out interesting information about the illustrator, not formal reports on when he was born and the like but rather such interesting information as is given in *Young Wings,* in publishers' catalogs, and in *The Junior Book of Authors, Writing Books for Boys and Girls,*[2] or *Illustrators of Children's Books, 1744-1945.*[3]

Compare the illustrations in the various books by this illustrator.

Discussions about authors. The dreaded "report" on an author's life should be avoided, but anything which the librarian or children themselves can offer about authors as real people will interest children.

The kind of information contained in *Young Wings,* the monthly magazine published by the Junior Literary Guild, 9 Rockefeller Plaza, New York, and in *Writing Books for Boys and Girls* appeals to children and provides good background material on authors and reasons for their writing certain books.

Children enjoy writing to their favorite authors, and authors usually answer their correspondence.

If there is a children's author in the community, ask him, or her, to come to the school to talk with the children.

Discussions about books in fields of children's interest. The librarian should discuss books with children frequently. Many a fine book remains unread on the library shelves because the children do not know about it.

Invite the children's librarian of the public library to visit the school and discuss books with the children.

Let children tell about interesting or unusual books they have discovered.

When a new bulletin board display or an exhibit of books is arranged, the librarian should take time to discuss the books briefly with the children.

New books always need to be introduced. A brief, descriptive sentence or two often is sufficient to arouse interest. New authors need special introductions. Familiar authors are welcomed by expectant readers.

Discussions about Newbery-Caldecott medal books. Display pictures of the Newbery and Caldecott medals on the bulletin board and explain about the awards.

---

[2] Young Wings, *Writing Books for Boys and Girls* (New York: Junior Literary Guild and Doubleday, 1952).

[3] Bertha E. Mahony, comp., *Illustrators of Children's Books, 1744-1945* (Boston: Horn Book, 1947).

Make a list of all the books which have received the medals and display those titles which are in the school library.

If the library funds are sufficient to enable the school to buy many of the new books of the year, let the children vote on which books they would suggest to receive the medals for that year.

Talks by librarian on history of books and bookmaking. Many children will find this type of discussion remote from their experiences and uninteresting. Others will be interested in the growth of the physical book from stone tablet to the modern machine product. The librarian must be sure of the interest of the group before she attempts this type of talk. Most children will be interested, however, in seeing the galley proof of a book, quarto pages, and the unmounted cover.

Reporting on books. One of the surest ways to destroy the child's natural delight in reading is to require him to report on a book when he has finished reading it. The book report that is simply a routine checkup on reading must be avoided. Most children, however, enjoy talking about books informally, and every school librarian is able to tell of some child's unusual reaction to reading which he has given to her at some odd moment. Such comments are interesting and worth while. They give real insight into the child's personality and assist the librarian in understanding children and in judging books for them.

Informal group discussions may center about books which the children are reading or have just completed. Some of the members of the group may wish to ask questions about the story or the characters. Older children may compare various books by the same author or discuss books on the same subject written by other authors. Children will call attention to the importance of the illustrations in the book. The important thing in these informal discussions is to maintain an atmosphere of sincerity in which children really express their personal opinions.

Many so-called "book reviews" are dull, tiresome, and boring. If oral reviews are given, they should have a clear-cut purpose. The whole purpose should be to awaken an interest in the book which might lead to a desire on the part of others to read it. The reviewer should acquaint the audience with the characters and perhaps with one or two high spots in the book. He may read aloud some particularly interesting section of the book, but if he does so it should be brief. He may recount some interesting anecdote about the author or how the book happened to be written. If the book is fiction, he definitely should not recount so much of the plot that he destroys the interest of those who wish to read the book later. In presenting an oral report, children should learn to announce clearly at the beginning the title and author of the book. If the illustrations are particularly notable, the illustrator's name may also be given.

After an oral review is finished, the audience should have an opportunity to evaluate it critically by considering such values as clarity, poise, sincerity, and manner of presentation. The reviewer should be expected to answer such questions from the audience as "Why did you choose the book to read?" "Is the story true?" "Did you learn anything new from the story?" "What part did you like best?" "Do you think that the solution is true-to-life?" and "Why do you recommend this particular book?" These and other key questions will arise when children are stimulated to think about books and judge them thoughtfully.

Formal, written book reviews which follow some form set by teacher or librarian have no place in the elementary school library program because they tend to destroy interest and pleasure in reading. Brief comments made by children during the discussion periods may be quoted and used on the bulletin board accompanying the book jacket as a means of selling the book to other readers. Children's comments, like the following, have real meaning:

The Bells on Finland Street by Lyn Cook:
> This is the story of a fairly poor girl who worked for what she wanted. When and how she got it is a wonderful story.—Barbara Sloate, H6th Grade.

Buffalo Bill by Frank L. Beals:
> An exciting book on how Wm. F. Cody earned his title of Buffalo Bill. He was the pride of the west.—Stephen Brandenburger, H6th Grade.

Buckskin by Thomas Hinkle:
> Buckskin is the story of a horse who leads a very rugged life. His mother is killed and he's left alone. If you read the book you will find what action packed stories Buckskin has.—Douglas Schwilk, L6th Grade.

Invisible Island by Dean Marshall:
> I liked the story of *Invisible Island* because the things that happened in it are more realistic than any other story I have read.— Margaret Weatherhead, H6th Grade.

Eddie and the Fire Engine by Carolyn Haywood:
> *Eddie and the Fire Engine* is a good book. I liked it when Eddie had the wrong hat and told the fireman that it was an old-time fire hat, but it was an opera hat!—Gregg Soligan, 5th Grade.

If the school has a newspaper, the library section will often consist of news about new books. Children should be given the opportunity to write the book notes for this section. Such notes or reviews have real meaning and often are the beginning of creative expression on the part of some child. The following notes written by children would be suitable for this purpose:

Carol from the Country by Frieda Friedman:
> I enjoyed the book *Carol from the Country* because it is an interesting family story. The Clarks, mother, father, Carol and the twins, moved from their pleasant country home to the noisy city. Carol disliked it very much. As you follow this story you will be filled with enjoyment from beginning to end.—Linda Hagopian, H6th Grade.

Lance and Cowboy Billy by Jack Holt and Carolyn Coggins:
> If you like cowboy stories you're sure to like this one. It is about two boys, Billy and Lance.
>
> Both boys had a horse. Billy's horse was named Sonny and Lance's horse was named Star.
>
> This story is readable and lifelike. It is not too artistic, but it has one picture in full color of the boys and their horses.
>
> This story takes place on the Flying A ranch, which Lance was visiting.—Fred Stephenson, 5th Grade.

Spot the Dalmatian Pup by Dorothy K. L'Hommedieu:
> Spot lived with her mother and her two little brothers on a big farm. Her family had many spots on their white coats, but Spot had only a few spots. Spot was very bad for she ate with the little pigs.
>
> She knew a pony named Jerry. The pony pulled a cart for the children on the farm and Spot raced along side. Spot liked Jerry very much. I hope you will too.—Janet Southard, H5th Grade.

After the Sun Sets by Miriam B. Huber:
> *The Princess on the Glass Hill* (from this book).
>
> I liked how much braver Boots was than his brothers. He stayed in the barn one night and his brothers were afraid to stay in there very long.

Boots found a horse and rode it to the top of the glass hill. Twice more he did the same thing, with two different horses. He won the princess.—Tony Mynsted, 5th Grade.

Mr. Flip Flop by Helen Garrett:

I think Mr. Flip Flop is a very humorous book. It also is an imaginative book.

It is about an old man who was a circus clown until he is too old to be one any more. He came to find a big red barn. He is a happy man when he buys the barn.—June Banta, H5th Grade.

King, the Story of a Sheep Dog by Thomas C. Hinkle:

The story begins when King was born. He then lived near a cattle ranch. When his mother and brothers are killed, he seeks shelter at the ranch. A few days later he is stolen from the ranch by a man called "Spanish Jim."

Spanish Jim hurt him while drunk and King lies by the river stunned. When he awoke he washed himself of blood, and went about looking for food.

He chased a rabbit into a hole and in a few seconds ran headlong into a wildcat.

Later a boy rescues him from the hole. From that time on he stayed with the boy until he is stolen.

In the end he returns to the boy and saves his life. It is, indeed, interesting to read of King's many adventures as a sheep dog.—Paul Clarke, 5th Grade.

Sharing through dramatizations

Children enjoy dramatizing scenes from books. A group of children who have read and enjoyed the same book may work together as a committee and present a scene from the book or present themselves as characters from the book. This type of presentation requires no scenery, little or no costuming, and practically no help on the part of the librarian. It is entirely pupil planned and executed. The librarian's main contribution will be to assist the group in selecting the scene for dramatization to be sure that only relatively simple scenes are attempted. No written parts are needed, but careful reading for details is essential so that spontaneity and naturalness of expression are forthcoming. Such dramatizations often take the form of radio or TV shows, with an announcer, sound effects, and other devices which add to the interest of the performance. The main purpose of the dramatization is to capture the interest of the group and convince the audience of what the book has to offer.

Discussions of radio and TV programs

See "The library in relation to radio and television," page 7, for the program discussions suggested there.

Storytelling and reading aloud

Children can enjoy and appreciate many books which are far beyond their ability to read or interpret for themselves. From the time children enter kindergarten until they leave school, they should have the opportunity to hear fine books read or to listen to stories. Storytelling and reading aloud will include a variety of literature— nonsense tales, poetry, fairy tales, short stories, hero tales, myths, legends, and fiction. It cannot be hoped that all children will enjoy all selections equally. Periods devoted to storytelling and reading aloud should be planned carefully, and the librarian should know her material thoroughly. The repetition of poems and stories develops familiarity and appreciation on the part of the children. The most gratifying response the librarian can receive at the close of a period of reading aloud or storytelling is a spontaneous "Read it again," or "Tell it again."

Storytelling is an art that requires study and preparation. Beautiful phrasing and interesting dialect should be retained in its original form. The storyteller will find it necessary to memorize parts of her selections in order to preserve the original flavor and beauty of the author's style. In storytelling there is direct communication between the narrator and the audience, providing an intimacy which is not present in reading aloud. The storyteller can look directly into the faces of the children without the interference of "the book." The best book on storytelling is Marie Shedlock's *The Art of the Storyteller,*[4] originally published in 1915 and now in its third edition.

The librarian will also want to make full use of audio-visual aids for the story hour. Fine radio and TV storytelling programs, records, and transcriptions bring the voices of outstanding storytellers to

---

[4] Marie Shedlock, *The Art of the Storyteller* (3d ed., rev.; New York: Dover Publications, 1951).

the library (*see* p.115). All such mediums contribute greatly to children's enjoyment of books, and the librarian has a responsibility to utilize them. They can form the basis for excellent group discussions.

Some stories are better read aloud than told, and reading aloud, if it is to be effective, requires careful preparation. An ordinary conversational tone is right for reading aloud, and practice will result in the ability to interpret dramatic passages in a natural manner. Reading should be slower than normal speaking, and a low, relaxed voice is the most pleasing. Unless pictures are large, clear, and easily seen when held up before a group, it is better to omit trying to show them while reading. If they are shown, it is important that there is enough light so that everyone can see them easily.

Poetry, especially, should be read to children. The enjoyment of poetry, however, depends greatly upon the way it is introduced. The librarian who loves poetry will have little trouble in getting the children to enjoy it. Her part is to select the poems wisely, read them well, and show her own interest and enthusiasm for them in her reading. The choice of selections should be guided by children's expressions of their interests, by the seasons of the year, and by timely events related to the lives of the children. Nonsense verse should have its place because of its innate appeal to children. It is never wise to attempt to analyze the verses, or ask the children to tell what the verses mean to them. Poetry's major appeal is emotional, and the enjoyment of it is too individual to expect that anyone can explain just what it means to him. Excellent suggestions on enjoying poetry with children and a fine collection of poems are contained in *Time for Poetry* by May Hill Arbuthnot.[5]

The period devoted to storytelling or reading aloud is most effective if the group is arranged in a very informal manner. Having the children near and informally seated permits the storyteller to speak in a natural tone of voice. The children themselves may be able to suggest the best seating arrangement for their own comfort and enjoyment during the period.

---

[5] May Hill Arbuthnot, *Time for Poetry* (Chicago: Scott, Foresman, 1951).

chapter 14

Instruction in the use of

books and libraries

An up-to-date elementary school library has a wide variety of materials and an extensive scope of services. In order that children may learn to utilize these materials and services, they need well-planned instruction in the use of books and libraries. Children do not know instinctively how to use indexes and tables of contents, how to find materials in an encyclopedia, or how to use the dictionary. They do not know where to look for specific kinds of information. They need instruction in the use of the card catalog. Without such instruction, even the best elementary school library is ineffective.

The amount and kind of library instruction to be given children depends somewhat upon the kind of library facilities available and the character of the educational program in the school. In a school with a large library and a creative type of curriculum, many library facilities are in active use. A single activity in one classroom may require the use of books, magazines, pamphlets, maps, pictures, charts, and graphs. The success of these materials in connection with the activity will depend upon how well the children are able to use them. Children need to know how to locate information, how to take notes, and how to condense and digest information which they find. The smaller the library, the more imperative it becomes that children know how to get the maximum use from the materials available.

Instruction in library and book usage should begin as soon as children begin to make use of books and library materials. All such instruction must be adapted to the children themselves and come out of real needs. The underlying aim of the instruction should be to help children gain independent habits of study and investigation so that they can use books independently and feel at home in a library.

There is some difference of opinion as to the most effective way to organize library instruction. Some librarians believe that it is best to give instruction only when specific problems arise; others believe that there should be a planned program of systematic training. The difficulty with the individual problem approach is that it is wasteful of the librarian's time and energy and leaves too much to chance. Under this plan many children would never become independent users of libraries. The difficulty with a too rigidly planned course of instruction is that it may become routine, isolated, and of no lasting value to children.

A well-planned program of library instruction includes both the approach through individual problems and systematic group instruction. It includes instruction given by both the classroom teacher and the librarian and may be carried on in both classroom and library. *(See* "How to use books and the library," p.148.) In order that there will be no wasteful duplication of instructional effort and that children may gain increasing skills, some definite plan for library instruction is recommended. Such instruction will be successful only if there is need for the particular information under discussion. All such needs grow out of classroom demands and there must be close cooperation between the librarian and classroom teacher so that techniques are taught at a time when classroom activities require their constant application.

There are only a few fundamentals that children need to know about using books and libraries.

They need to know that:

Books are arranged in a library according to a system as an aid to the user of the library.

Books are shelved numerically from left to right and section by section.

Shelf labels are guides to books on those particular shelves.

The card catalog is an index on cards of all books in the library. It records books according to author, title, and subject.

Various parts of a book have distinctive and important uses.

They need to know how to:

Find books in a library through use of the card catalog.

Interpret graphs and charts.

Use encyclopedias and dictionaries and understand what kinds of information they contain.

Use special reference books.

Take notes.

Make and use bibliographies.

The amount and complexity of the information children need about books and libraries increase as they progress from grade to grade. There are practical ways of teaching children what they need to know on their particular levels of understanding. Many school systems provide manuals or courses of study which outline the program of library instruction according to grades. The following outline for grades three and four illustrates a typical plan for organized library instruction.[1]

PROMOTING LIBRARY USE: TEACHING THE USE OF BOOKS AND LIBRARIES

III. Grade 3

A. Review suggestions outlined in Grades 1 and 2.

B. Introduce the technique of finding books.
1. Teach the location of easy books.
2. Explain the "E" on the back of the book.
3. Teach the letters of the alphabet—which are in the beginning, which are towards the end and which are near the center.
4. Teach authors and titles.
5. Introduce author initial on the "E" books.
6. Teach location of books on shelves.
7. Practice returning books to their proper places on the shelves.

C. Introduce books other than story books.

D. Encourage the child to use judgment in choice of reading.

E. Try to lengthen the span of interest.

F. Teach the use of the table of

---

[1] Department of Public Instruction, Territory of Hawaii, *Hawaii School Libraries: A Manual for Organization and Activities* (Honolulu, T. H.: The Department, 1951).

contents to locate a story in a book.

G. Show the difference between chapters and short stories.

H. Create an appreciation and understanding of the public library—storytelling activities, displays, etc., if the school is near a branch or main library, or has bookmobile service.

I. Show how torn pages are mended, soiled books cleaned, etc.

IV. Grade 4

A. Review material outlined in Grade 3.

B. Encourage the use of the public library.

Borrow books and pictures for classroom activities and arrange for classes to make visits to the public library.

C. Teach children how to locate books on shelves, emphasizing the following points:

1. Each book belongs on a particular shelf and in a particular place on the shelf.

2. Shelves in the library are named Fiction, Science, Fairy Tales, History, etc.

3. All books are named in some way, either by a number or a letter, as
   "F"—Fiction
   "E"—Easy books
   822—Plays
   398—Fairy tales
   591—Animal stories

4. Numbers go around the shelves, beginning with 000's to the 900's so that a book with the number 591 comes before the number 592.

D. Teach children how to return books to the right shelf when browsing.

E. Teach children how to locate a desired book by means of a knowledge of the classification system.

F. Teach the ten main divisions and important sub-divisions.

G. Teach the use of shelf guides.

H. Use activities and devices to emphasize the subject arrangement of books.

I. Simple use of the card catalog may be taught to advanced fourth grade groups; see under Grades 5 and 6.

J. Teach parts of a book.

1. Construction of book
   Method of assembling book
   Value of this type of book construction

2. Name and definition of each part
   a. Cover
   b. Frontispiece
   c. Title page
   d. Copyright date page
   e. Dedication page
   f. Introduction, foreword or preface
   g. Table of contents
   h. List of illustrations
   i. Text—or body of the book
   j. Bibliography
   k. Glossary
   l. Notes
   m. Appendix
   n. Index

The amount of time which will be required to carry on library instruction is an important consideration. The individual instruction comes about naturally in the child's ordinary use of the library, but some specific time needs to be set aside for group instruction. It has been observed as a matter of practice that a half-hour a week is quite adequate for group instruction, providing the program of instruction is well organized.

An excellent book written for children and one which is being used successfully as a supplementary textbook in teaching the use of books and libraries is *The Children's Book on How to Use Books and Libraries* by Carolyn Mott and Leo Baisden.[2] The book grew out of library lessons used in an elementary school over a period of five years. The accompanying *Lesson Book* is also useful. The material in the book is easily adapted to any program of teaching library usage set up by individual schools, since it discusses all phases of library techniques useful to children. Carefully worked-out tests are included in the *Lesson Book,* although the final test of the acquisition of such knowledge comes from the ability to use the knowledge gained.

Citizenship and care of books

Desirable citizenship is not difficult to obtain within the library. It results automatically when attitudes of courtesy, consideration, cooperation, and responsibility in the individual child are developed. The need for strict formality disappears as these attitudes become more and more a part of the child's daily life. Each child needs to feel responsible for the general appearance of the library and co-operate by leaving chairs, tables, books, and shelves in correct arrangement for the children who are to come next to use the library. Discipline problems do not need to develop. A low speaking voice on the part of both librarian and children is a prime factor in obtaining the informality so vital to the friendly atmosphere of the library.

The librarian needs to take time to make children aware of the intrinsic as well as the monetary value of the book collection. Fine editions, new books, expensive reference sets, and beautiful illus-

---

[2] Carolyn Mott and Leo B. Baisden, *The Children's Book on How to Use Books and Libraries* (New York: Scribner, 1948).

trations, if called to the children's attention, will aid in their consideration and feeling of responsibility toward books. The beauty of the library itself and the pleasure derived by the children in using all the library facilities are important factors in the development of wholesome citizenship attitudes.

Guidance in handling books must be given by the librarian as soon as children begin to use the library. Primary children who have used the public library or who have received instruction from their teachers on care of books come to the library as well-prepared citizens, but many children come with no former training in the care of books. They must learn why clean hands are essential. They must learn that pages are turned from the upper right-hand corner with "dry" fingers and that small, thin slips of paper make the best bookmarks. They will need instruction in the proper handling of oversize books, so that the bottoms of pages do not become frayed and torn. They must learn that proper shelving of books is a necessary part of good care. They must understand that care in shelving avoids torn pages and broken bindings and that books should always be placed on the shelves with the right side up and the spine facing out. These understandings are important. They are a part of good, library citizenship.

chapter 15

The library in the
primary grades

In the primary grades children's library activities will of necessity be centered in the classroom, and the responsibility for carrying on the activities will fall primarily upon the classroom teacher. In this respect the situation differs markedly from the middle and upper grades where library activities center more in the school library.

The success of the library in the primary grades depends both upon the teacher's ability to carry on an active program of library activities and upon an administrative organization which provides for effective cooperation between the classroom teacher and the school librarian.

A modern program of primary teaching calls for the wide use of books of various types. The library has contributions to make to children from the moment they enter school. Even before they have learned to read, the use of picture books forms a strong background for prereading training and reading interest. As soon as children have learned to read the simple preprimers, there is a field of books which they can use successfully. The ordinary primary reading program provides mainly for instruction in reading skills, but the teacher must look to the library to furnish children more extensive opportunity to use the reading skills they are acquiring.

There is an exceptionally fine field of books available for young children. There are the many beautiful picture books which may

The traveling library brings
new experiences.

Just one more chapter, please.

be used in the kindergarten and first grade to interest children in learning to read. There are the lovely books which the teacher may use for the story hour. There are the photographic picture books and well-illustrated books on factual subjects which can contribute greatly to furthering class activities. There are books written so simply that even the beginning reader thrills over his ability to "read a whole book." Even some of the newer sets of readers have primary books which are written so interestingly and illustrated so attractively that children enjoy reading them for pleasure. Books! books! books! and the primary children need them all.

Young children respond immediately to a good story and clamor for more at the end of the story hour. They like to look at gay pictures and take keen pleasure in recognizing and reading familiar words. Often, too, it is by reading a familiar story or by showing the lovely pictures of some familiar tale that the primary teacher is able to bring children, books, and herself into happy acquaintance and friendly relationship. It is seldom that the primary teacher finds a child entirely lacking in interest in books, yet often she finds children in whom she must develop an interest in the reading of books. Where a lack of interest does exist it is usually due to the fact that the child is not ready to read, and the teacher must help him to develop a background for reading. The use of books plays a very important part in developing a reading background and in stimulating an interest in reading.

A library corner

The mere accessibility of reading materials is a powerful incentive to reading, and no modern primary room is complete without its "Library," "Library Corner," or "Library Table." This corner may easily be provided in any primary classroom at very little expense. A real library atmosphere can be achieved by the addition of a few shelves, a bulletin board, a table and chairs, and a collection of attractive books. (*See* "The Library Corner in the Classroom," p.52.)

The library books for the primary rooms should be a part of the book collection of the main school library and should be checked out to teachers to provide the book collections for the library corners. The books should be changed frequently in order to keep them fresh and interesting and in order to provide for the various interests and abilities of the children. The teacher should keep in close touch with the school librarian in order to be familiar with all books and materials which are available.

LIBRARY ACTIVITIES FOR PRIMARY GRADES

A definite time should be set aside each day for children to participate in library activities, otherwise there is little reason to set up a library corner. The habit of allowing children to use the library corner only when they finish their assigned work defeats the purpose entirely. Under this plan slow children may never have an opportunity to enjoy books because many of them are unable to complete normal assignments. Often these same children profit greatly from time spent in looking at books and in enjoying them with their friends. Primary library activities should include not only activities in the classroom but also an occasional opportunity to visit the school library in order to see special exhibits, to enjoy storytelling by the librarian, or just to get acquainted with the library. (*See* "Promoting Library Use," Grade 3, p.140.)

Recreational reading

Library activities in the primary grades are as varied as in the middle and upper grades. Perhaps the most important of all library activities are the activities which pertain to recreational reading. Even in the primary grades, children should be given time to read just for the fun of reading. They need to experience the pleasure that comes from browsing through books and from reading about favorite pets or pastimes. It is only through constant association with books that children can come to know the enjoyment books give. The child finds these values for himself if he is surrounded with books on various subjects, simple enough for him to read, and if he is given opportunity to browse through and read the books of his own particular choice. When he is reading for recreation, he must be given freedom to select the books *he* wants to read. His particular interests will show up very soon, and these interests are of great help to the teacher in her understanding of the child. Through recreational reading the child actually puts into practice the techniques of reading he has been acquiring. He is increasing his ability to read by practicing the art of reading. He is increasing his speed in reading by reading more. He is acquiring the habit of reading the way he acquires other habits—by experience and repetition. He is increasing his vocabulary, expanding his interests, and enlarging his horizons. He is, in fact, learning to read by reading.

Reading guidance

Children should have some time each day for recreational reading. Some children will have difficulty in selecting the book they want to read, and it becomes the teacher's job to assist them in finding just the right book. The suggestions given in Chapter 11, "Reading guidance and library activities," will be useful to the primary teacher. Even primary children must have the feeling that they themselves are making the final selection of what they are to read. The teacher gives them ideas about the various books and stories, but the final choice is theirs. The better readers often know well in advance what they want to read. They browse more successfully than do the poor readers, and they keep in mind certain stories they have seen or heard about. They often have more varied interests than do the poor readers and books on many subjects appeal to them. Also, they are more likely to discuss their books informally together and get ideas from each other about what to read next. The good reader needs very little help from the teacher in making his selections for recreational reading. The good reader who has had freedom in selecting books soon becomes an independent user of the library so far as his recreational reading is concerned. To assist the poor reader successfully with his selections for recreational reading requires tact, ingenuity, sympathy, and real understanding.

Citizenship and care of books

From the time children begin to use books, they need direction and help in the care of books. Young children often consider books merely as playthings and will do nothing more than turn pages and look at pictures hastily, casting the book aside when the last page is turned, only to snatch another book and repeat the process. Wrong habits can be avoided if right attitudes towards books are stressed from the beginning. Primary children soon learn that books are different from their toys. They should be taught the proper care and handling of them, how to turn pages, how to mark one's place, why clean hands are important when using books, why returning books to their proper places is a good idea. They soon take great pride in caring for the library. Courtesy and respect for others in the use of books and other library materials comes to have real meaning. The pages of oversize books will become torn at the bottom from rubbing against woolly sweaters unless children are shown that this can be avoided by laying the book flat on the table and turning the pages from the upper right-hand corner. It is easy to establish good book and library habits by the end of the third grade. It requires patience, skill, and constant attention on the part of the teacher when children are using library materials, but children willingly cooperate when they understand the "why" of things.

How to use books and the library

Library lessons or lessons on how to use books and library materials begin with the child's first use of books. The amount of instruction the child actually needs in the primary grades is not great, yet it is very important. The first-grade child must be shown that pages are numbered, why they are numbered, where to look for the page number, and how to find pages by number. This knowledge is needed with the first use of preprimers. Also, with the use of the first preprimer, the child must be shown the advantages of turning pages from the upper right-hand corner with dry fingers. He must be shown how to shelve books properly according to whatever plan is used. He must even learn that large picture books are placed with the front of the book facing up so that the title can be read.

By the beginning of the fourth grade, children should have a fair knowledge of the alphabet, since this forms the basis for all library usage. If third-grade classes make use of the main school library room, children will need to be shown the sections of books in the library which they will use most. They must learn the purpose of shelf labels. They learn that all books on the same subject are shelved together, and that all books are shelved alphabetically by the last name of the author. This knowledge will require that they understand the fact that the author's name is always given on the title page. They soon discover for themselves that the title page also is the place where they can always find the title of the book. Thus the title page of a book comes to have meaning and use to the third grader. Social studies work in the third grade may require that children be shown the table of contents as a means of knowing what the book is about.

Classroom activities may require the use of pictures or pamphlet material. For example, a third-grade class may be working on a unit centering around life on the farm. Pictures and pamphlets are needed. A child is sent to the library to get pictures and pamphlets about farm life. This request gives the child his introduction to the pamphlet file. The librarian shows him the huge drawers he has so often wondered about. She withdraws the pamphlets and pictures about farm life. She may help him to make a selection of materials. He returns to the classroom with the material plus an enthusiastic story about how "this material is kept in those big drawers called the pamphlet file." Now the pamphlet file becomes a reference source for that particular class, and thus third graders learn of its importance.

Discussion periods

Primary children need opportunities to share their reading experiences with one another, and this can be accomplished best through informal discussion periods. During these periods the place of the teacher or librarian is that of a member of the group contributing her ideas along with those of the children. The activities for this period are varied. Many of the suggestions in Chapter 13, "Sharing reading experiences," can be readily adapted for use in the primary grades.

Storytelling

Storytelling and reading aloud by the teacher or librarian are very important library activities in the primary grades. Although the subject of storytelling is presented in the chapter on sharing reading experiences, it seems pertinent to emphasize the subject here as it relates to the primary children.

The child's first experiences with books and stories are controlled by some adult. The child is read to or he listens to stories selected by an adult. Unless the stories appeal to the child, this activity can become so dull and boring that he may form a distaste for stories and books in general. In selecting stories for primary children, one should give thought especially to the content. Stories will appeal to the younger children more if they are about something they have actually experienced, if they are about familiar things they know and understand. Small children, too, enjoy stories with much repetition of words and phrases, for they are highly sensitive to rhythm. They enjoy participation stories and will enter wholeheartedly into the spirit of the story. Second and third graders begin to see the difference between the factual and the fanciful stories and will enjoy the simple folk and fairy tales. Poems which tie in with the children's experiences will be most enjoyed. If the content of the poem is understood, children will get enjoyment from unrimed and blank verse quite as well as from rimed, metrical verse.

The manner of presenting a story to children greatly affects their interest in it. The group must be arranged in an informal and un-crowded manner, and it is important that the children be able to see the face of the storyteller and that she be able to see theirs. Many stories are better read than told, for the rhythm of some stories is gone with the altering of even a few words or phrases. Whether she reads or tells the story, the storyteller should know her story well. She must learn the value of pauses, and while some gestures are natural and add interest to the story she must strive to avoid all exaggerated and superficial gestures and facial expressions.

Many radio story hours are planned for the primary age child, and excellent records are available also. There is difference of opinion about the use of such mediums for storytelling to small children. Many teachers and librarians use both radio and records with real success. Others insist that children of this age get more enjoyment from actually seeing the storyteller as she tells the story and that radio or record presentations lack the human warmth and companionship so essential to small children. Television storytelling programs for small children have proved highly successful because of the presence of the storyteller, and perhaps this medium soon will be utilized in the classroom and school library for the story hour. Most teachers and librarians agree that TV has great potentialities in the realm of storytelling.

SELECTING LIBRARY BOOKS
FOR PRIMARY CHILDREN

The task of selecting books for primary children is both interesting and difficult. The field of children's books grows steadily year by year, and librarians and teachers must be reviewing and reading new materials constantly in order to be able to select books wisely. Fine book lists have been compiled by authorities in the primary field and these aid greatly in book selection. A list of good book lists appears in Chapter 7, "Selecting books and magazines." However, there is no substitute for the actual reading of books as a basis for selection. The task is not a task for either the teachers or the librarian alone. It is rather a cooperative task which requires all primary teachers in a school to work with the librarian in suggesting books for purchase. The librarian is likely to have a wider knowledge of the field of books available on the various subjects, but the teachers know what types of books they need for their particular classes and activities.

The school library seeks to provide primary children with books for recreational reading and also with books which will assist them with their classroom activities. The choice of material which first graders can read by themselves is limited. At the second-grade level more books are available, and by the time children reach the third-grade level of reading ability the field of books is wide and varied. Gradually more books are appearing in the primary field, and there are now available quite a number of short, simply written little books which have the appearance of "real books." There are books on every subject which might interest the modern child. There are farm stories, animal stories, fairy stories, folktales, books about airplanes, ships, trains, and automobiles—all simply written and beautifully illustrated. For young children, also, there are many fine picture books and easy books which appear in the various dime stores. Excellent book lists evaluating these inexpensive books are available and can be used as guides in selection. Two of these are given on page 74.

Another type of book which has an important place in the primary grades is the picture book. This type of book is increasing in number every year. Publishers, authors, and illustrators vie with each other in producing books fine in content and artistic in appearance. Many of these books cannot actually be read by primary children, but they appeal to them and make excellent material for the teacher to read aloud. They are useful, too, in connection with classroom activities. Some of them can be enjoyed by children of all ages, even by adults, and it is not unusual to find a section of a high school library devoted to a group of modern picture books for children. Many of these books represent the finest examples of bookmaking, but they are expensive. Children need the experience of such books, but they should be used under the guidance of the teacher. No school can afford to buy large numbers of expensive books for classroom use, but, regardless of price, primary children should be given the privilege of living with and enjoying beautiful picture books.

Out of the many books published for young children, it is the task of the teachers and librarians to select the best in each field. The standards for selecting children's books are discussed in Chapter 7, "Selecting books and magazines." These same standards apply to the selection of all books for children. Teachers and librarians selecting books for primary children must apply these standards to every book they select.

chapter **16**

The school library and
the public library

There was a time when some educators and librarians felt that there was a distinct conflict between the aims of the school library and the aims of the children's department of the public library. It was contended that the school library should be organized and conducted primarily to serve instructional needs, and that it should be the function of the public library to care for the recreational reading needs of young people. Experience in many cities where both progressive schools and progressive public libraries are to be found has established beyond question the fact that there is no essential conflict between the school library and the children's department of the public library. Both librarians and educators are realizing today that the task of providing adequate library service to meet all of the book needs of modern childhood taxes the best efforts of both the school library and the public library—that each may supplement the other and that each is able to perform some services which the other is not in a position to perform.[1]

A common aim

Public libraries are continuing to develop and expand their children's departments and many of them are maintaining a separate

---

[1] The influence of the public library on the development of school libraries is described by Mildred L. Batchelder in "Public Library Influence on School Libraries," *Library Trends,* I (January 1953), 271-85.

department for older boys and girls. This department is planned for young people of high school and college age and is giving more effective service to young people than either the adult department or the children's department was able to give previously. In large public libraries such a department serves also to bridge the gap between the children's department and the adult department. The function of any department of the public library which serves young people and the function of the modern school library are essentially the same—the bringing of books and young people together in a constant and happy relationship so that from the moment children begin to use books they may have an understanding and appreciation of the joys and privileges that may come from books and reading.

Certain conditions may be regarded as essential for successful cooperation between the public library and the school library. The first prerequisite is mutual understanding and acquaintance. The school librarian and the librarian in charge of children's work in the public library need to know each other. The school librarian needs to visit the children's department frequently to keep herself informed about the activities which are going on. She needs to know the book collection which is available to the children and needs to "keep up" with the new books which are purchased from time to time.

Likewise, the librarian of the children's department is an important factor in the education of the child, and part of her job is to keep abreast of developments in the field of education. She needs to understand the school and its developing program so that she can serve the children better. To get this understanding she must become acquainted with the school librarian and the teachers and discuss with them their common problems. She needs to visit the school library and, if possible, visit classrooms and teachers in order to understand the educational program. She should be invited to attend special meetings of school librarians or teachers, and her possible contributions as a guest speaker to such groups should not be overlooked. Friendly relationships almost invariably bring about mutual understanding. There are no two fields more closely allied for a common purpose than the school library and the children's department of the public library.

Public library and school library working together

There is a definite obligation on the part of the school librarian to lead children to use the wide facilities and services of the public library. Although children patronize the public library voluntarily, the school librarian may do much to stimulate the early formation of the habit of using the public library. The most successful school reading program is one which carries over into the public library. The school library can never supply the variety and scope of materials which the public library provides. The two libraries can aid each other, and definite plans for cooperation need to be worked out between them. There are various ways of achieving this cooperation. Some plans may be very successful in one community and not so satisfactory in others, but it should be noted that there are certain concrete ways through which the two libraries can work together and give each other help.

The public library aids the school by—

Providing for frequent visits of the children's librarian to the school. Her program of activities will include talks about the services of the public library. She may make out library cards for children and explain how to use them. She may tell stories, read aloud, or discuss books in general. Her visits help her to develop a friendly relationship with the children.

Distributing regular bulletins to schools giving news of the children's department, lists of new books, special bibliographies related to holidays or other timely events.

Maintaining a traveling library or bookmobile service to schools which are located far from the public library or from one of its branches.

Planning summer reading projects.

Supplementing the school library book collection with special collections of books. These are either sent direct to the school library or to individual classroom teachers.

Maintaining book collections for home circulation in schools which are in isolated sections of the community far from the public library.

Cooperating with school committees in compiling book lists and bibliographies on special subjects.

Providing expert assistance in book selection for school libraries. This is especially important where there is no trained personnel in charge of school library service.

Assisting school authorities with plans for organizing and establishing school libraries. This is very necessary in small communities where there is no one with library training in the school department. Some public libraries have taken full charge of purchasing and organizing the original book collection in school libraries.

Providing for the reading needs of children all through the year. Most school libraries are closed on Saturdays and during the summer vacation so that children would be entirely without book service a good part of their free time if it were not for the public library.

Providing books for home circulation. The book collections of most school libraries are too small to provide for home circulation.

The school library aids the public library by—

Making more intelligent users of the public library through a planned program of instruction in the use of books and libraries.

Implanting the "library idea" in many children whom the public library would never otherwise reach.

Giving wide publicity to all activities of the children's department of the public library.

Interesting children in the location of the public library and its branches and in the varied services it offers to its patrons.

Introducing children to the public library or its branches through class visits to the children's room.

Providing exhibits of children's art work which pertain to books or reading activities for display in the public library.

Providing for most of the reference needs of the children.

Index